THE FIRST INDIAN WAR OF INDEPENDENCE 1857 - 1859

THE FIRST INDIAN WAR OF INDEPENDENCE 1857 - 1859

KARL MARX, FREDERICK ENGELS

GYAN

Published by

Gyan Publishing House
5, Ansari Road
Daryaganj, New Delhi-110002
Phone: 011-47034999, 9811692060
E-mail: books@gyanbooks.com

Distribution Network
gyanbooks.com
India, USA, Canada, UK, Australia

ISBN: 978-93-7225-094-7 (HB)

2nd Impression 2025

Printed at: Gyan Press, Delhi.

THE FIRST INDIAN WAR OF INDEPENDENCE 1857 - 1859
Author: KARL MARX, FREDERICK ENGELS

The First Indian War of Independence 1857 1859

Karl Marx

The First Indian War of Independence 1857-1859

CONTENTS*

* The titles of the articles given by the Institute of Marxism-Leninism of the C.C. C.P.S.U. are marked by an asterisk. – *Ed.*

Introduction

The bulk of the present collection is made up of articles written by Karl Marx and Frederick Engels for the *New-York Daily Tribune* on the 1857-59 national-liberation revolt in India. The collection also contains articles written by Marx in 1853 on the situation in India on the eve of the revolt, extracts from his *Notes on Indian History*, and from letters containing important passages by the founders of Marxism on the insurrection.

Since the early eighteen-fifties Marx and Engels had always shown great interest in the colonial policy of capitalist countries and the national-liberation struggle of oppressed nations. They studied the history of Eastern countries, especially that of the colonial and dependent countries of Asia, principally India and China.

The historical destiny of the latter two great countries, objects of a predatory capitalist colonial policy, engaged Marx and Engels above all from the standpoint of the proletarian liberation struggle. They regarded the revolutionary impact of the far-reaching changes maturing in India and China with the dissolution of patriarchal and feudal relations and the gradual transition of those countries to capitalist development, as a new important factor that would inevitably influence the prospects of the impending European revolution. This explains why Marx and Engels followed the Indian insurrection which broke out in the spring of 1857 with such concentration. They reacted to all the major events of the insurrection, dealing at length in their articles with its causes, the reasons for its defeat, the fighting, and its historical impact. The insurrection, they held, was part and parcel of the general anti-colonial liberation struggle of oppressed nations unfolding in the eighteen-fifties nearly in all Asia. They saw that it was allied to the European revolution which, in their opinion, was due to break out as a sequel of the first world economic crisis which swept the European countries and the United States at that time.

The collection opens with Marx's articles, "The British Rule in India," "The East India Company — Its History and Results," and "The Future Results of the British Rule in India," written in connection with a fresh revision in 1853 by the British Parliament of the Charter of the East India Company. Based on a thorough study of numerous authorities on Indian history, these articles vividly illustrate Marx's irreconcilable opposition to colonialism, and belong by rights to his best works on the national-colonial question. In fact they reveal the economic and political premises which had made the insurrection of 1857 inevitable.

In these articles Marx presents a profound scientific analysis of the conquest and enslavement of India and notes the variety of forms and methods of British colonial rule and exploitation. He describes the East India Company as the tool of Indian conquest and stresses that it seized Indian territories in predatory wars by taking advantage of the feudal strife between local princes and fanning racial, religious, tribal and caste antagonisms among the peoples of India.

Marx demonstrates that the colonial plunder of India — one of the principal sources of enrichment for the ruling oligarchy in Britain — caused the collapse of entire branches of the Indian economy and the extreme impoverishment of the people of that vast, wealthy and ancient country. The British intruders, he notes, neglected public works and thus brought about the collapse of India's irrigated agriculture. They doomed millions of Indians to starvation by breaking up local industries, notably the hand-weaving and the hand-spinning, which could not hope to compete with the British cotton fabrics flooding the Indian market. The colonialists broke down the patriarchal framework of communal landownership. At the same time, however, by introducing successively two land-tax and tenure systems — the zamindari and ryotwari — they preserved many feudal survivals in the Indian social system, which slowed down that country's progressive development and burdened the Indian peasantry.

The British authorities in India burdened the ryot peasant with unbearable taxes, putting him thus under the double yoke of the local feudal aristocracy and the colonial state. In his articles of 1853 and his series of articles on the Indian revolt, Marx notes that the Indian peasant had to bear an extremely heavy tax burden, extortion, violence and cruel torture applied everywhere by the tax collector. Torture came to be an officially recognized organic institution of Britain's financial policy in India ("Investigation of Tortures in India", "The Indian Revolt", "Taxes in India", etc.). Yet no part of the taxes collected was returned to the people in public works, which are more indispensable in Asiatic countries than anywhere else, Marx stresses.

Marx draws the conclusion that it was the predatory policy of the British intruders in India and the barbarous methods of colonial exploitation which nurtured the Indian revolt.

The immediate causes which precipitated the insurrection were bound up closely by Marx and Engels with the changes that took shape in India under British rule by the mid-19th century, particularly in the functions of the native army. The principle of "divide and rule" had helped Britain to conquer India and to rule it for a century and a half with practically no major upheavals. But by the mid-19th century the circumstances of their domination changed appreciably, Marx wrote. The East India Company had by then completed her territorial conquests and was well installed in the country as its sole conqueror. To keep the Indian people in submission, the Company looked for support to her native army, whose main purpose changed from military to police functions to keep down the conquered population. Marx observes that a population of 200 million was thus kept in submission by a native army of 200,000 officered by Englishmen and kept in check by an English force of 40,000. But in creating the native army, the British in India "simultaneously organised the first general centre of resistance which the Indian people was ever possessed of." (See p. 38 of this collection.) This is precisely why, Marx concludes, the general insurrection was not begun by the hunger-stricken pilfered ryots, but by the privileged well-paid sepoys —the men and officers of the native regiments of the Anglo-Indian army recruited preponderantly from the higher Indian castes. It had been an article of faith with the English that the sepoy army constituted their whole strength in India, and they were rudely awakened to the fact that that very army constituted the main source of danger for them ("Dispatches from India").

Marx points out, however, that the sepoys were little more

than the tools ("The Indian Question"). The principal motive power behind the insurrection were the people of India, who rallied to the struggle against the unbearable colonial oppression. Marx and Engels refuted the false contention of the British ruling classes, who tried to picture the insurrection as an armed sepoy mutiny and to conceal the involvement in it of broad sections of the Indian population. The authors described the movement from the first as a national revolt — a revolution of the Indian people against British rule ("The Revolt in the Indian Army", "The Revolt in India", and others, and "Notes on Indian History"). Marx and Engels laid special emphasis on the revolt bringing together not only people of different religions (Hindus and Moslems) and castes (Brahmins, Rajputs and, in some cases, Sikhs) but also of different social standing. "It is the first time," Marx wrote, "that sepoy regiments have murdered their European officers; that Mussulmans and Hindus, renouncing their mutual antipathies, have combined against their common masters; that 'disturbances beginning with the Hindus, have actually ended in placing on the throne of Delhi a Mohammedan emperor'; that the mutiny has not been confined to a few localities." (See p. 38 of this collection.)

Although the British press did its all to hush up the participation in the revolt of the people's masses, Marx asserted in his early articles that the Indian people not only sympathized with, but supported, the revolt in every way. In his "The Indian Revolt" Marx proved beyond doubt that broad sections of the people — the peasants most of all — took part in the insurrection in a direct or indirect way. The immense scale of the revolt, Marx wrote, and the fact that the English met great difficulties in obtaining supplies and transports for their troops, witnessed to the hostility of the Indian peasantry.

In "The Annexation of Oudh", "Lord Canning's Proclamation and Land Tenure in India" and other articles, Marx stressed that the policy of forcible British expansion through the annexation of the still independent Indian territories and the confiscation of land belonging to native principalities had also been one of the immediate causes of the revolt. The population in the annexed territories suffered great hardships. A large section of India's propertied classes was outraged. The British refused to honour agreements which had for decades governed their relations with the local princes. They annexed independent Indian territories in violation of officially recognized treaties. This and the confiscation of Indian principalities whenever a native prince died without natural heirs roused the Indian feudal landowners.

Anti-British sentiment was also rife at the time of the revolt among the Indian bourgeoisie—a fact corroborated by the failure of the Indian war loan undertaken by the East India Company in Calcutta.

Marx and Engels had every sympathy for the liberation struggle of the Indian people. They hoped that the revolt would triumph. Yet they knew that its success depended on whether or not all sections of India's population, particularly in South and Central India, would render it all-round support. However, there had been no such general action, and for a number of historical reasons: the feudal division of India, the ethnic diversity of its population, the religious and caste antagonisms among the people, and the perfidy of most of the local feudal gentry who had led the revolt.

Marx and Engels considered the absence of a single centralized insurrectionist leadership and a single military command to have been one of the principal reasons for the failure of the insurrection. The same applies to internal strife and dissent in the rebel camp. Inferior military strength and lack of experience in waging war against a well-equipped European army also told fatally on the outcome of the revolt. The intrinsic pattern of the revolt was unstable: it reduced the chances of success in the military operations, and told deplorably on rebel morale. It created confusion among the rebels and led ultimately to their defeat ("The Capture of Delhi", "The Capture of Lucknow", "Details of the Attack on Lucknow"). However, Marx and Engels note, the insurrectionists put up a brave fight in face of all hardships and disadvantages, especially at the principal points of the uprising—Delhi and Lucknow. Although defeated in the defence of Delhi, they demonstrated the full force of the national revolt which, Engels observed, did not come to the fore as much in regular battle as in guerrilla warfare.

In a number of their articles Marx and Engels furnish an annihilating description of the "civilized" British colonial army, its brutal treatment of defeated insurrectionists and the looting of captured rebel towns and villages.

In estimating the historical impact of the Indian revolt, Marx points out that while it failed to alter the colonial regime in India to any appreciable extent, it revealed the general hatred among the Indian people of colonial enslavement, and showed its ability and determination for liberation. The revolt had compelled the British colonialists to change somewhat their forms and methods of colonial rule. Among other things, they abolished the East India Company, whose policy outraged opinion in India.

Steadfast fighters against colonialism, Marx and Engels always had faith in the liberation of the Indian people from colonial slavery. Marx pointed out that the development of productive forces in India as a result of British rule would fail to improve the lot of the Indian people as long as the latter did not put an end to foreign colonial oppression and become master of its own country. Marx saw two ways of achieving this goal — a proletarian revolution in Britain or a liberation struggle of the Indian people itself against the domination of foreign colonialists. "The Indians," Marx wrote, "will not reap the fruits of the new elements of society scattered among them by the British bourgeoisie, till in Great Britain itself the now ruling classes shall have been supplanted by the industrial proletariat, or till the Hindus themselves shall have grown strong enough to throw off the English yoke altogether." (See p. 33 of this collection.)

The people of India marked the centennial of the 1857-59 revolt in circumstances when the prophecy of the great proletarian leader about India's liberation from colonialism had come true. India has won its national independence in resolute and drawn-out struggle against colonial oppression and stands today firmly on the road of independent national development.

Institute of Marxism-Leninism
of the C.C. C.P.S.U.

K. Marx

THE BRITISH RULE IN INDIA[1]

London, Friday, June 10, 1853

Telegraphic dispatches from Vienna announce that the pacific solution of the Turkish, Sardinian and Swiss questions,[2] is regarded there as a certainty.

Last night the debate on India[3] was continued in the House of Commons, in the usual dull manner. Mr. Blackett charged the statements of Sir Charles Wood and Sir J. Hogg with bearing the stamp of optimist falsehood. A lot of ministerial and Directorial[4] advocates rebuked the charge as well as they could, and the inevitable Mr. Hume summed up by calling on ministers to withdraw their bill. Debate adjourned.

Hindustan is an Italy of Asiatic dimensions, the Himalayas for the Alps, the Plains of Bengal for the Plains of Lombardy, the Deccan for the Appenines, and the Isle of Ceylon for the Island of Sicily. The same rich variety in the products of the soil, and the same dismemberment in the political configuration. Just as Italy has, from time to time, been compressed by the conqueror's sword into different national masses, so do we find Hindustan, when not under the pressure of the Mohammedan, or the Mogul, or the Briton, dissolved into as many independent and conflicting states as it numbered towns, or even villages. Yet, in a social point of view, Hindustan is not the Italy, but the Ireland of the East. And this strange combination of Italy and of Ireland, of a world of voluptuousness and of a world of woes, is anticipated in the ancient traditions of the religion of Hindustan. That religion is at once a religion of sensualist exuberance, and a religion of self-torturing asceticism; a religion of the Lingam, and of the Juggernaut; the religion of the Monk, and of the Bayadere.

I share not the opinion of those who believe in a golden age of Hindustan, without recurring, however, like Sir Charles Wood, for the confirmation of my view, to the authority of Kuli Khan.[5] But take, for example, the times of Aurungzeb; or the epoch, when the Mogul appeared in the North, and the Portuguese in the South; or the age of Mohammedan invasion, and of the Heptarchy[6] in Southern India; or, if you will, go still more back to antiquity, take the mythological chronology of the Brahmin himself, who places the commencement of Indian misery in an epoch even more remote than the Christian creation of the world.

There cannot, however, remain any doubt but that the misery inflicted by the British on Hindustan is of an essentially different and infinitely more intensive kind than all Hindustan had to suffer before. I do not allude to European despotism, planted upon Asiatic despotism, by the British East India Company, forming a more monstrous combination than any of the divine monsters startling us in the Temple of Salsette. This is no distinctive feature of British colonial rule, but only an imitation of the Dutch, and so much so that in order to characterize the working of the British East India Company, it is sufficient to literally repeat what Sir Stamford Raffles, the *English* Governor of Java, said of the old Dutch East India Company.

> "The Dutch Company, actuated solely by the spirit of gain, and viewing their subjects with less regard or consideration than a West India planter formerly viewed a gang upon his estate, because the latter had paid the purchase money of human property, which the other had not, employed all the existing machinery of despotism to squeeze from the people their utmost mite of contribution, the last dregs of their labour, and thus aggravated the evils of a capricious and semi-barbarous Government, by working it with all the practised ingenuity of politicians, and all the monopolizing selfishness of traders."

All the civil wars, invasions, revolutions, conquests, famines, strangely complex, rapid and destructive as the successive action in Hindustan may appear, did not go deeper than its surface. England has broken down the entire framework of Indian society, without any symptoms of reconstitution yet appearing. This loss of his old world, with no gain of a new one, imparts a particular kind of melancholy to the present misery of the Hindu, and separates Hindustan, ruled by Britain, from all its ancient traditions, and from the whole of its past history.

There have been in Asia, generally, from immemorial times, but three departments of Government: that of Finance, or the plunder of the interior: that of War, or the plunder of the exterior; and, finally, the department of Public Works. Climate and territorial conditions, especially the vast tracts of desert, extending from the Sahara, through Arabia, Persia, India and Tartary, to the most elevated Asiatic highlands, constituted artificial irrigation by canals and waterworks the basis of Oriental agriculture. As in Egypt and India, inundations are used for fertilizing the soil in Mesopotamia, Persia, etc.; advantage is taken of a high level for feeding irrigative canals. This prime necessity of an economical and common use of water, which, in the Occident, drove private enterprises to voluntary association, as in Flanders and Italy, necessitated in the Orient where civilization was too low and the territorial extent too vast to call into life voluntary association, the interference of the centralizing power of Government. Hence an economical function devolved upon all Asiatic Governments, the function of providing public works. This artificial fertilization of the soil, dependent on a Central Government, and immediately decaying with the neglect of irrigation and drainage, explains the otherwise strange fact that we now find whole territories barren and desert that were once brilliantly cultivated, as Palmyra, Petra, the ruins in Yemen, and large provinces of Egypt, Persia and Hindustan; it also explains how a single war of devastation has been able to depopulate a country for centuries, and to strip it of all its civilization.

Now, the British in East India accepted from their predecessors the department of finance and of war, but they have neglected entirely that of public works. Hence the deterioration of an agriculture which is not capable of being conducted on the British principle of free competition, of *laissez faire* and *laissez aller.*[7] But in Asiatic empires we are quite accustomed to see agriculture deteriorating under one government and reviving again under some other government. There the harvests correspond to good or bad governments, as they change in Europe with good or bad seasons. Thus the oppression and neglect of agriculture, bad as it is, could not be looked upon as the final blow dealt to Indian society by the British intruder, had it not been attended by a circumstance of quite different importance, a novelty in the annals of the whole Asiatic world. However changing the political aspect of India's past must appear, its social condition has remained unaltered since its remotest antiquity, until the first decennium of the 19th century. The hand-loom and the spinning-wheel, producing their regular myriads of spinners and weavers, were the pivots of the structure of that society. From immemorial times, Europe received the admirable textures of Indian labour, sending in return for them her precious metals, and furnishing thereby this material to the goldsmith, that indispensable member of Indian society, whose love of finery is so great that even the lowest class, those who go about nearly naked, have commonly a pair of golden ear-rings and a gold ornament of some kind hung round their necks. Rings on the fingers and toes have also been common. Women as well as children frequently wore massive bracelets and anklets of gold or silver and statuettes of divinities in gold and silver were met with in the households. It was the British intruder who broke up the Indian hand-loom and destroyed the spinning-wheel. England began with driving the Indian cottons from the European market; it then introduced twist into Hindustan and in the end inundated the very mother country of cotton with cottons. From 1818 to 1836 the export of twist from Great Britain to India rose in the proportion of 1 to 5,200. In 1824 the export of British muslins to India hardly amounted to 1,000,000 yards, while in 1837 it surpassed 64,000,000 yards. But at the same time the population of Dacca decreased from 150,000 inhabitants to 20,000. This decline of Indian towns celebrated for their fabrics was by no means the worst consequence. British steam and science uprooted over the whole surface of Hindustan, the union between agriculture and manufacturing industry.

These two circumstances—the Hindu, on the one hand, leaving, like all Oriental peoples, to the Central Government the care of the great public works, the prime condition of his agriculture and commerce, dispersed, on the other hand, over the surface of the country, and agglomerated in small centres by the domestic union of agricultural and manufacturing pursuits—these two circumstances had brought about, since the remotest times, a social system of particular features—the so-called *village system*, which gave to each of these small unions their independent organization and distinct life. The peculiar character of this system may be judged from the following description, contained in an old official report of the British House of Commons on Indian affairs:

"A village, geographically considered, is a tract of country comprising some hundred or thousand acres of arable and waste lands; politically viewed it resembles a corporation or township. Its proper establishment of officers and servants consists of the following descriptions: The *potail* or head inhabitant, who has generally the superintendence of the affairs of the village, settles the disputes of the inhabitants, attends to the police, and performs the duty of collecting the revenue within his village, a duty which his personal influence and minute acquaintance with the situation and concerns of the people render him the best qualified for this charge. The *kurnum* keeps the accounts of cultivation, and registers everything connected with it. The *tallier* and the *totie*, the duty of the former of which consists in gaining information of crimes and offences, and in escorting and protecting persons travelling from one village to another; the province of the latter appearing to be more immediately confined to the village, consisting, among other duties, in guarding the crops and assisting in measuring them. The *boundaryman*, who preserves the limits of the village, or gives evidence respecting them in cases of dispute. The superintendent of tanks and watercourses distributes the water for the purposes of agriculture. The Brahmin, who performs the village worship. The schoolmaster, who is seen teaching the children in a village to read and write in the sand. The calendar-Brahmin, or astrologer, etc. These officers and servants generally constitute the establishment of a village; but in some parts of the country it is of less extent; some of the duties and functions above described being united in the same person; in others it exceeds the above-named number of individuals. Under this simple form of municipal government, the inhabitants of the country have lived from time immemorial. The boundaries of the villages have been but seldom altered; and though the villages themselves have been sometimes injured, and even desolated by war, famine or disease, the same name, the same limits, the same interests, and even the same families, have continued for ages. The inhabitants gave themselves no trouble about the breaking up and divisions of kingdoms; while the village remains entire, they care not to what power it is transferred, or to what sovereign it devolves; its internal economy remains unchanged. The potail is still the head inhabitant, and still acts as the petty judge or magistrate, and collector or rentor of the village."[8]

These small stereotype forms of social organism have been to the greater part dissolved, and are disappearing, not so much through the brutal interference of the British tax-gatherer and the British soldier, as to the working of English steam and English Free Trade. Those family-communities were based on domestic industry, in that peculiar combination of hand-weaving, hand-spinning and hand-tilling agriculture which gave them self-supporting power. English interference having placed the spinner in Lancashire and the weaver in Bengal, or sweeping away both Hindu spinner and weaver, dissolved these small semi-barbarian, semi-civilized communities, by blowing up their economical basis, and thus produced the greatest, and, to speak the truth, the only *social* revolution ever heard of in Asia.

Now, sickening as it must be to human feeling to witness those myriads of industrious patriarchal and inoffensive social organizations disorganized and dissolved into their units, thrown into a sea of woes, and their individual members losing at the same time their ancient form of civilization and their hereditary means of subsistence, we must not forget that these idyllic village communities, inoffensive though they may appear, had always been the solid foundation of Oriental despotism, that they restrained the human mind within the smallest possible compass, making it the unresisting tool of superstition, enslaving it beneath traditional rules, depriving it of all grandeur and historical energies. We must not forget the barbarian egotism which, concentrating on some miserable patch of land, had quietly witnessed the ruin of empires, the perpetration of unspeakable cruelties, the massacre of the population of large towns, with no other consideration bestowed upon them than on natural events, itself the helpless prey of any aggressor who deigned to notice it at all. We must not forget that this undignified, stagnatory, and vegetative life, that this passive sort of existence evoked on the other part, in contradistinction, wild, aimless, unbounded forces of destruction, and rendered murder itself a religious rite in Hindustan. We must not forget that these little communities were contaminated by distinctions of caste and by slavery, that they subjugated man to external circumstances instead of elevating man to be the sovereign of circumstances, that they transformed a selfdeveloping social state into never changing natural destiny, and thus brought about a brutalizing worship of nature, exhibiting its degradation in the fact that man, the sovereign of nature, fell down on his knees in adoration of Hanuman, the monkey, and Sabbala, the cow.

England, it is true, in causing a social revolution in Hindustan, was actuated only by the vilest interests, and was stupid in her manner of enforcing them. But that is not the question. The question is, can mankind fulfil its destiny without a fundamental revolution in the social state of Asia? If not, whatever may have been the crimes of England she was the unconscious tool of history in bringing about that revolution.

Then, whatever bitterness the spectacle of the crumbling of an ancient world may have for our personal feelings, we have the right, in point of history, to exclaim with Goethe:

"Sollte diese Qual uns quälen,
Da sie unsre Lust vermehrt,

*Hat nicht Myriaden Seelen Timurs Herrschaft aufgezehrt?"**

Written by K. Marx on June 10, 1853.
Published in the *New-York Daily Tribune*, No. 3804, of June 25, 1853.
Signed: *Karl Marx*

Printed according to the newspaper text

---

* *Should this torture then torment us*
Since it brings us greater pleasure?
Were not through the rule of Timur
Souls devoured without measure?

From Goethe's *Westostlicher Diwan*, "An Suleika". —*Ed.*

K. Marx

THE EAST INDIA COMPANY — ITS HISTORY AND RESULTS

London, Friday, June 24, 1853

The debate on Lord Stanley's motion to postpone legislation for India, has been deferred until this evening. For the first time since 1783 the Indian question has become a ministerial one in England. Why is this?

The true commencement of the East India Company cannot be dated from a more remote epoch than the year 1702, when the different societies, claiming the monopoly of the East India trade, united together in one single Company. Till then the very existence of the original East India Company was repeatedly endangered, once suspended for years under the protectorate of Cromwell, and once threatened with utter dissolution by parliamentary interference under the reign of William III. It was under the ascendancy of that Dutch Prince when the Whigs became the farmers of the revenues of the British Empire, when the Bank of England sprung into life, when the protective system was firmly established in England, and the balance of power in Europe was definitively settled, that the existence of an East India Company was recognized by Parliament. That era of apparent liberty was in reality the era of monopolies not created by Royal grants, as in the times of Elizabeth and Charles I, but authorized and nationalized by the sanction of Parliament. This epoch in the history of England bears, in fact, an extreme likeness to the epoch of Louis Philippe in France, the old landed aristocracy having been defeated, and the bourgeoisie not being able to take its place except under the banner of moneyocracy, or the "haute finance." The East India Company excluded the common people from the commerce with India, at the same time that the House of Commons excluded them from parliamentary representation. In this as well as in other instances, we find the first decisive victory of the bourgeoisie over the feudal aristocracy coinciding with the most pronounced reaction against the people, a phenomenon which has driven more than one popular writer, like Cobbett, to look for popular liberty rather in the past than in the future.

The union between the Constitutional Monarchy and the monopolizing moneyed interest, between the Company of East India and the "glorious" revolution of 1688[9] was fostered by the same force by which the liberal interests and a liberal dynasty have at all times and in all countries met and combined, by the force of corruption, that first and last moving power of Constitutional Monarchy, the guardian angel of William III and the fatal demon of Louis Philippe. So early as 1693, it appeared from parliamentary inquiries, that the annual expenditure of the East India Company, under the head of "gifts" to men in power, which had rarely amounted to above £1,200 before the revolution, reached the sum of £90,000. The Duke of Leeds was impeached for a bribe of £5,000, and the virtuous King himself convicted of having received £10,000. Besides these direct briberies, rival Companies were thrown out by tempting Government with loans of enormous sums at the lowest interest, and by buying off rival Directors.

The power the East India Company had obtained by bribing the Government, as did also the Bank of England, it was forced to maintain by bribing again, as did the Bank of England. At every epoch when its monopoly was expiring, it could only effect a renewal of its Charter by offering fresh loans and by fresh presents made to the Government.

The events of the Seven Years' war[10] transformed the East India Company from a commercial into a military and territorial power. It was then that the foundation was laid of the present British Empire in the East. Then East India stock rose to £263, and dividends were then paid at the rate of 12½ per cent. But then there appeared a new enemy to the Company, no longer in the shape of rival societies, but in the shape of rival ministers and of a rival people. It was alleged that the Company's territory had been conquered by the aid of British fleets and British armies, and that no British subjects could hold territorial sovereignties independent of the Crown. The ministers of the day and the people of the day claimed their share in the "wonderful treasures" imagined to have been won by the last conquests. The Company only saved its existence by an agreement made in 1767 that it should annually pay £ 400,000 into the National Exchequer.

But the East India Company, instead of fulfilling its agreement, got into financial difficulties, and, instead of paying a tribute to the English people, appealed to Parliament for pecuniary aid. Serious alterations in the Charter were the consequence of this step. The Company's affairs failing to improve, notwithstanding their new condition, and the English nation having simultaneously lost their colonies in North America, the necessity of elsewhere regaining some great Colonial Empire became more and more universally felt. The illustrious Fox thought the opportune moment had arrived, in 1783, for bringing forward his famous Indian bill, which proposed to abolish the Courts of Directors and Proprietors, and to vest the whole Indian government in the hands of seven Commissioners appointed by Parliament. By the personal influence of the imbecile King* over the House of Lords, the bill of Mr. Fox was defeated, and made the instrument of breaking down the then Coalition Government of Fox and Lord North, and of placing the famous Pitt at the head of the Government. Pitt carried in 1784 a bill through both Houses, which directed the establishment of the Board of Control, consisting of six members of the Privy Council, who were

> "to check, superintend and control all acts, operations and concerns which in any wise related to the civil and military government, or revenues of the territories and possessions of the East India Company."

On this head, Mill, the historian, says:

> "In passing that law two objects were pursued. To avoid the imputation of what was represented as the heinous object of Mr. Fox's bill, it was necessary that the principal part of the power should *appear* to remain in the hand of the Directors. For ministerial advantage it was necessary that it should in reality be all taken away. Mr. Pitt's bill professed to differ from that of his rival, chiefly in this very point, that while the one destroyed the power of the Directors, the other left it almost entire. Under the act of Mr. Fox the powers of the ministers would have been avowedly held. Under the act of Mr. Pitt, they were held in secret and by fraud. The bill of Fox transferred the power of the Company to Commissioners appointed by Parliament. The bill of Mr. Pitt transferred them to Commissioners appointed by the King."[11]

---

* George III. —*Ed.*

The years of 1783 and 1784 were thus the first, and till now the only years, for the Indian question to become a ministerial one. The bill of Mr. Pitt having been carried, the Charter of the East India Company was renewed, and the Indian question set aside for twenty years. But in 1813 the Anti-Jacobin war,[12] and in 1833 the newly introduced Reform Bill[13] superseded all other political questions.

This, then, is the first reason of the Indian question's having failed to become a great political question, since and before 1784; that before that time the East India Company had first to conquer existence and importance; that after that time the oligarchy absorbed all of its power which it could assume without incurring responsibility; and that afterwards the English people in general were at the very epochs of the renewal of the Charter, in 1813 and at 1833, absorbed by other questions of overbearing interest.

We will now take a different view. The East India Company commenced by attempting merely to establish factories for their agents, and places of deposit for their goods. In order to protect them they erected several forts. Although they had, even as early as 1689, conceived the establishment of a dominion in India, and of making territorial revenue one of their sources of emolument, yet, down to 1744, they had acquired but a few unimportant districts around Bombay, Madras, and Calcutta. The war which subsequently broke out in the Carnatic had the effect of rendering them after various struggles, virtual sovereigns of that part of India. Much more considerable results arose from the war in Bengal and the victories of Clive. These results were the real occupation of Bengal, Bihar, and Orissa. At the end of the 18th century, and in the first years of the present one, there supervened the wars with Tippoo Sahib, and in consequence of them a great advance of power, and an immense extension of the subsidiary system.[14] In the second decennium of the 19th century the first convenient frontier, that of India within the desert, had at length been conquered. It was not till then that the British Empire in the East reached those parts of Asia, which had been, at all times, the seat of every great central power in India. But the most vulnerable point of the Empire, from which it had been overrun as often as old conquerors were expelled by new ones, the barriers of the Western frontier, were not in hands of the British. During the period from 1838 to 1849, in the Sikh and Afghan wars, British rule subjected to definitive possession the ethnographical, political, and military frontiers of the East Indian continent, by the compulsory annexation of the Punjab and of Scinde.[15] These were possessions indispensable to repulse any invading force issuing from Central Asia, and indispensable against Russia advancing to the frontiers of Persia. During this last decennium there have been added to the British Indian territory 167,000 square miles, with a population of 8,572,630 souls. As to the interior, all the native states now became surrounded by British possessions, subjected to British *suzeraineté* under various forms, and cut off from the seacoast, with the sole exception of Gujarat and Scinde. As to its exterior, India was now finished. It is only since 1849, that the one great Anglo-Indian Empire has existed.

Thus the British Government has been fighting, under the Company's name, for two centuries, till at last the natural limits of India were reached. We understand now, why during all this time all parties in England have connived in silence, even those which had resolved to become the loudest with their hypocritical peace-cant, after the *arrondissement* of the one Indian Empire should have been completed. Firstly, of course, they had to get it, in order to subject it afterward to their sharp philanthropy. From this view we understand the altered position of the Indian question in the present year, 1853, compared with all former periods of Charter renewal.

Again, let us take a different view. We shall still better understand the peculiar crisis in Indian legislation, on reviewing the course of British commercial intercourse with India through its different phases.

At the commencement of the East India Company's operations, under the reign of Elizabeth, the Company was permitted for the purpose of profitably carrying on its trade with India, to export an annual value of £30,000 in silver, gold, and foreign coin. This was an infraction against all the prejudices of the age, and Thomas Mun was forced to lay down in *A Discourse of Trade, from England unto the East-Indies*[16] the foundation of the "mercantile system", admitting that the precious metals were the only real wealth a country could possess, but contending at the same time their exportation might be safely allowed, provided the *balance of payments* was in favour of the exporting nation. In this sense, he contended that the commodities imported from East India were chiefly reexported to other countries, from which a much greater quantity of bullion was obtained than had been required to pay for them in India. In the same spirit, Sir Josiah Child wrote *A Treatise Wherein Is Demonstrated I. That the East-India Trade Is the Most National of All Foreign Trades.*[17] By-and-by the partisans of the East India Company grew more audacious, and it may be noticed as a curiosity, in this strange Indian history, that the Indian monopolists were the first preachers of free trade in England.

Parliamentary intervention, with regard to the East India Company, was again claimed, not by the commercial, but by the industrial class, at the latter end of the 17th century, and during the greater part of the 18th, when the importation of East Indian cotton and silk stuffs was declared to ruin the poor British manufacturers, an opinion put forward in John Pollexfen's *England and East-India Inconsistent in Their Manufactures*; London, 1697,[18] a title strangely verified a century and a half later, but in a very different sense. Parliament did then interfere. By the Act 11 and 12 William III, Cap. 10, it was enacted that the wearing of wrought silks and of printed or dyed calicoes from India, Persia and China should be prohibited, and a penalty of £200 imposed on all persons having or selling the same. Similar laws were enacted under George I, II and III, in consequence of the repeated lamentations of the afterward so "enlightened" British manufacturers. And thus, during the greater part of the 18th century, Indian manufactures were generally imported into England in order to be sold on the Continent, and to remain excluded from the English market itself.

Besides this parliamentary interference with East India, solicited by the greedy home manufacturer, efforts were made at every epoch of the renewal of the Charter, by the merchants of London, Liverpool and Bristol, to break down the commercial monopoly of the Company, and to participate in that commerce, estimated to be a true mine of gold. In consequence of these efforts, a provision was made in the Act of 1773 prolonging the Company's Charter till March 1, 1814, by which private British individuals were authorized to export from, and the Company's Indian servants permitted to import into, England almost all sorts of commodities. But this concession was surrounded with conditions annihilating its effects, in respect to the exports to British India by private merchants. In 1813 the Company was unable to further withstand the pressure of general commerce, and except the monopoly of the Chinese trade, the trade to India was opened, under certain conditions, to private competition. At the renewal of the Charter in 1833, these last restrictions were at length superseded, the Company forbidden to carry on any trade at all—their commercial character destroyed and their privilege of excluding British subjects from the Indian territories withdrawn.

Meanwhile the East Indian trade had undergone very serious revolutions, altogether altering the position of the different class interests in England with regard to it. During the whole course of the 18th century the treasures transported from India to England were gained much less by comparatively insignificant commerce, than by the direct exploitation of that country, and by the colossal fortunes there extorted and transmitted to England. After the opening of the trade in 1813 the commerce with India more than trebled in a very short time. But this was not all. The whole character of the trade was changed. Till 1813 India had been chiefly an exporting country, while it now became an importing one; and in such a quick progression, that already in 1823 the rate of exchange, which had generally been 2/6 per rupee, sunk down to 2/per rupee. India, the great workshop of cotton manufacture for the world, since immemorial times, became now inundated with English twists and cotton stuffs. After its own produce had been excluded from England, or only admitted on the most cruel terms, British manufactures were poured into it at a small and merely nominal duty, to the ruin of the native cotton fabrics once so celebrated. In 1780 the value of British produce and manufactures amounted only to £386,152, the bullion exported during the same year to £15,041, the total value of exports during 1780 being £12,648,616, so that the Indian trade amounted to only 1/32 of the entire foreign trade. In 1850 the total exports to India from Great Britain and Ireland were £8,024,000 of which cotton goods alone amounted to £5,220,000, so that it reached more than 1/8 of the whole export, and more than 1/4 of the foreign cotton trade. But, the cotton manufacture also employed now 1/8 of the population of Britain, and contributed 1/12 of the whole national revenue. After each commercial crisis the East Indian trade grew of more paramount importance for the British cotton manufacturers, and the East Indian continent became actually their best market. At the same rate at which the cotton manufactures became of vital interest for the whole social frame of Great Britain, East India became of vital interest for the British cotton manufacture.

Till then the interests of the moneyocracy which had

converted India into its landed estates of the oligarchy who had conquered it by their armies, and of the millocracy who had inundated it with their fabrics, had gone hand in hand. But the more the industrial interest became dependent on the Indian market, the more it felt the necessity of creating fresh productive powers in India, after having ruined her native industry. You cannot continue to inundate a country with your manufactures, unless you enable it to give you some produce in return. The industrial interest found that their trade declined instead of increasing. For the four years ending with 1846, the imports to India from Great Britain were to the amount of 261 million rupees; for the four years ending 1850 they were only 253 millions, while the exports for the former period, 274 millions of rupees, and for the latter period, 254 millions. They found out that the power of consuming their goods was contracted in India to the lowest possible point, that the consumption of their manufactures by the British West Indies, was of the value of about 14s. per head of the population per annum, by Chile, of 9s. 3d., by Brazil of 6s. 5d., by Cuba, of 6s. 2d., by Peru of 5s. 7d., by Central America of 10d., while it amounted in India only to about 9d. Then came the short cotton crop in the United States, which caused them a loss of £11,000,000 in 1850, and they were exasperated at depending on America, instead of deriving a sufficiency of raw cotton from the East Indies. Besides, they found that in all attempts to apply capital to India they met with impediments and chicanery on the part of the Indian authorities. Thus India became the battle-field in the contest of the industrial interest on the one side, and of the moneyocracy and oligarchy on the other. The manufacturers, conscious of their ascendency in England, ask now for the annihilation of these antagonistic powers in India, for the destruction of the whole ancient fabric of Indian government, and for the final eclipse of the East India Company.

And now to the fourth and last point of view, from which the Indian question must be judged. Since 1784 Indian finances have got more and more deeply into difficulty. There exists now a national debt of 50 million pounds, a continual decrease in the resources of the revenue, and a corresponding increase in the expenditure, dubiously balanced by the gambling income of the opium tax, now threatened with extinction by the Chinese beginning themselves to cultivate the poppy, and aggravated by the expenses to be anticipated from the senseless Burmese war.[19]

"As the case stands," says Mr. Dickinson, "as it would ruin England to lose her Empire in India, it is stretching our own finances with ruin, to be obliged to keep it."[20]

I have shown thus, how the Indian question has become for the first time since 1783, an English question, and a ministerial question.

Written by K. Marx on June 24, 1853.
Published in the *New-York Daily Tribune*, No. 3816, of July 11, 1853.
Signed: *Karl Marx*.

Printed according to the newspaper text

K. Marx

THE FUTURE RESULTS OF THE BRITISH RULE IN INDIA

London, Friday, July 22, 1853

I propose in this letter to conclude my observations on India.

How came it that English supremacy was established in India? The paramount power of the Great Mogul was broken by the Mogul Viceroys. The power of the Viceroys was broken by the Mahrattas.[21] The power of the Mahrattas was broken by the Afghans, and while all were struggling against all, the Briton rushed in and was enabled to subdue them all. A country not only divided between Mohammedan and Hindu, but between tribe and tribe, between caste and caste; a society whose framework was based on a sort of equilibrium, resulting from a general repulsion and constitutional exclusiveness between all its members. Such a country and such a society, were they not the predestined prey of conquest? If we knew nothing of the past history of Hindustan, would there not be the one great and incontestable fact, that even at this moment India is held in English thraldom by an Indian army maintained at the cost of India? India, then, could not escape the fate of being conquered, and the whole of her past history, if it be anything, is the history of the successive conquests she has undergone. Indian society has no history at all, at least no known history. What we call its history, is but the history of the successive intruders who founded their empires on the passive basis of that unresisting and unchanging society. The question, therefore, is not whether the English had a right to conquer India, but whether we are to prefer India conquered by the Turk, by the Persian, by the Russian, to India conquered by the Briton.

England has to fulfil a double mission in India: one destructive, the other regenerating—the annihilation of old Asiatic society, and the laying of the material foundations of Western society in Asia.

Arabs, Turks, Tartars, Moguls, who had successively overrun India, soon became *Hinduized*, the barbarian conquerors being, by an eternal law of history, conquered themselves by the superior civilization of their subjects. The British were the first conquerors superior, and, therefore, inaccessible to Hindu civilization. They destroyed it by breaking up the native communities, by uprooting the native industry, and by levelling all that was great and elevated in the native society. The historic pages of their rule in India report hardly anything beyond that destruction. The work of regeneration hardly transpires through a heap of ruins. Nevertheless it has begun.

The political unity of India, more consolidated, and extending farther than it ever did under the Great Moguls, was the first condition of its regeneration. That unity, imposed by the British sword, will now be strengthened and perpetuated by the electric telegraph. The native army, organized and trained by the British drill-sergeant, was the *sine qua non* of India self-emancipation, and of India ceasing to be the prey of the first foreign intruder. The free press, introduced for the first time into Asiatic society, and managed principally by the common offspring of Hindus and Europeans, is a new and powerful agent of reconstruction. The zemindari and ryotwari[22] themselves, abominable as they are, involve two distinct forms of private property in land —the great desideratum of Asiatic society. From the Indian natives, reluctantly and sparingly educated at Calcutta, under English superintendence, a fresh class is springing up, endowed with the requirements for government and imbued with European science. Steam has brought India into regular and rapid communication with Europe, has connected its chief ports with those of the whole southeastern ocean, and has revindicated it from the isolated position which was the prime law of its stagnation. The day is not far distant when, by a combination of railways and steam vessels, the distance between England and India, measured by time, will be shortened to eight days, and when that once fabulous country will thus be actually annexed to the Western world.

The ruling classes of Great Britain have had, till now, but an accidental, transitory and exceptional interest in the progress of India. The aristocracy wanted to conquer it, the moneyocracy to plunder it, and the millocracy to undersell it. But now the tables are turned. The millocracy have discovered that the transformation of India into a reproductive country has become of vital importance to them, and that, to that end, it is necessary, above all, to gift her with means of irrigation and of internal communication. They intend now drawing a net of railroads over India. And they will do it. The results must be inappreciable.

It is notorious that the productive powers of India are paralyzed by the utter want of means for conveying and exchanging its various produce. Nowhere, more than in India, do we meet with social destitution in the midst of natural plenty, for want of the means of exchange. It was proved before a Committee of the British House of Commons, which sat in 1848, that

"when grain was selling from 6s. to 8s. a quarter at Khandesh, it was sold 64s. to 70s. at Poona, where the people were dying in the streets of famine, without the possibility of gaining supplies from Khandesh, because the clay roads were impracticable."

The introduction of railroads may be easily made to subserve agricultural purposes by the formation of tanks, where ground is required for embankment, and by the conveyance of water along the different lines. Thus irrigation, the *sine qua non* of farming in the East, might be greatly extended, and the frequently recurring local famines, arising from the want of water, would be averted. The general importance of railways, viewed under this head, must become evident, when we remember that irrigated lands, even in the districts near Ghats, pay three times as much in taxes, afford ten or twelve times as much employment, and yield twelve or fifteen times as much profit, as the same area without irrigation.

Railways will afford the means of diminishing the amount and the cost of the military establishments. Col. Warren, Town Major of the Fort St. William, stated before a Select Committee of the House of Commons:

"The practicability of receiving intelligence from distant parts of the country in as many hours as at present it requires days and even weeks, and of sending instructions with troops and stores, in the more brief period, are considerations which cannot be too highly estimated. Troops could be kept at more distant and healthier stations than at present, and much loss of life from sickness would by this means be spared. Stores could not to the same extent be required at the various depots, and the loss by decay, and the destruction incidental to the climate, would also be avoided. The number of troops might be diminished in direct proportion to their effectiveness."

We know that the municipal organization and the economical basis of the village communities have been broken up, but their worst feature, the dissolution of society into stereotype and disconnected atoms, has survived their vitality. The village isolation produced the absence of roads in India, and the absence of roads perpetuated the village isolation. On this plan a community existed with a given scale of low conveniences, almost without intercourse with other villages, without the desires and efforts indispensable to social advance. The British having broken up this self-sufficient *inertia* of the villages, railways will provide the new want of communication and intercourse. Besides,

"one of the effects of the railway system will be to bring into every village affected by it such knowledge of the contrivances and appliances of other countries, and such means of obtaining them, as will first put the hereditary and stipendiary village artisanship of India to full proof of its capabilities, and then supply its defects." (Chapman, *The Cotton and Commerce of India*.)[23]

I know that the English millocracy intend to endow India with railways with the exclusive view of extracting at diminished expenses the cotton and other raw materials for their manufactures. But when you have once introduced machinery into the locomotion of a country, which possesses iron and coals, you are unable to withhold it from its fabrication. You cannot maintain a net of railways over an immense country without introducing all those industrial processes necessary to meet the immediate and current wants of railway locomotion, and out of which there must grow the application of machinery to those branches of industry not immediately connected with railways. The railway system will therefore become, in India, truly the forerunner of modern industry. This is the more certain as the Hindus are allowed by British authorities themselves to possess particular aptitude for accommodating themselves to entirely new labour, and acquiring the requisite knowledge of machinery. Ample proof of this fact is afforded by the capacities and expertness of the native engineers in the Calcutta mint, where they have been for years employed in working the steam machinery, by the natives attached to the several steam-engines in the Hardwar coal districts, and by other instances. Mr. Campbell himself, greatly influenced as he is by the prejudices of the East India Company, is obliged to avow

"that the great mass of Indian people possesses a great *industrial energy*, is well fitted to accumulate capital, and remarkable for a mathematical clearness of head, and talent for figures and exact sciences." "Their intellects," he says, "are excellent."[24]

Modern industry, resulting from the railway system, will dissolve the hereditary divisions of labour, upon which rest the Indian castes, those decisive impediments to Indian progress and Indian power.

All the English bourgeoisie may be forced to do will neither emancipate nor materially mend the social condition of the mass of the people, depending not only on the development of the productive powers, but on their appropriation by the people. But what they will not fail to do is to lay down the material premises for both. Has the bourgeoisie ever done more? Has it ever effected a progress without dragging individuals and peoples through blood and dirt, through misery and degradation?

The Indians will not reap the fruits of the new elements of society scattered among them by the British bourgeoisie, till in Great Britain itself the now ruling classes shall have been supplanted by the industrial proletariat, or till the Hindus themselves shall have grown strong enough to throw off the English yoke altogether. At all events, we may safely expect to see, at a more or less remote period, the regeneration of that great and interesting country, whose gentle natives are, to use the expression of Prince Saltykov, even in the most inferior classes, "*plus fins et plus adroits que les Italiens*,"* whose submission even is counterbalanced by a certain calm nobility, who, notwithstanding their natural languor, have astonished the British officers by their bravery, whose country has been the source of our languages, our religions, and who represent the type of the ancient German in the Jat and the type of the ancient Greek in the Brahmin.

I cannot part with the subject of India without some concluding remarks.

The profound hypocrisy and inherent barbarism of bourgeois civilization lies unveiled before our eyes, turning from its home, where it assumes respectable forms, to the colonies, where it goes naked. They are the defenders of property, but did any revolutionary party ever originate agrarian revolutions like those in Bengal, in Madras, and in Bombay? Did they not, in India, to borrow an expression of that great robber, Lord Clive himself, resort to atrocious extortion, when simple corruption could not keep pace with their rapacity? While they prated in Europe about the inviolable sanctity of the national debt, did they not confiscate in India the dividends of the rajahs, who had invested their private savings in the Company's own funds? While they combated the French revolution under the pretext of defending

* "More subtle and adroit than the Italians." Marx quotes from A. D. Saltykov's book *Lettres sur l'Inde*, Paris, 1848, p. 61. —*Ed.*

"our holy religion," did they not forbid, at the same time, Christianity to be propagated in India, and did they not, in order to make money out of the pilgrims streaming to the temples of Orissa and Bengal, take up the trade in the murder and prostitution perpetrated in the temple of Juggernaut? These are the men of "Property, Order, Family, and Religion".

The devastating effects of English industry, when contemplated with regard to India, a country as vast as Europe, and containing 150 millions of acres, are palpable and confounding. But we must not forget that they are only the organic results of the whole system of production as it is now constituted. That production rests on the supreme rule of capital. The centralization of capital is essential to the existence of capital as an independent power. The destructive influence of that centralization upon the markets of the world does but reveal, in the most gigantic dimensions, the inherent organic laws of political economy now at work in every civilized town. The bourgeois period of history has to create the material basis of the new world — on the one hand the universal intercourse founded upon the mutual dependency of mankind, and the means of that intercourse; on the other hand the development of the productive powers of man and the transformation of material production into a scientific domination of natural agencies. Bourgeois industry and commerce create these material conditions of a new world in the same way as geological revolutions have created the surface of the earth. When a great social revolution shall have mastered the results of the bourgeois epoch, the market of the world and the modern powers of production, and subjected them to the common control of the most advanced peoples, then only will human progress cease to resemble that hideous pagan idol, who would not drink the nectar but from the skulls of the slain.

Written by K. Marx on July 22, 1853.
Published in the *New-York Daily Tribune*, No. 3840, of August 8, 1853.
Signed: *Karl Marx*.

Printed according to the newspaper text

K. Marx

THE REVOLT IN THE INDIAN ARMY[25]

The Roman *divide et impera* was the great rule by which Great Britain, for about one hundred and fifty years, contrived to retain the tenure of her Indian Empire. The antagonism of the various races, tribes, castes, creeds and sovereignties the aggregate of which forms the geographical unity of what is called India, continued to be the vital principle of British supremacy. In later times, however, the conditions of that supremacy have undergone a change. With the conquest of Scinde and the Punjab, the Anglo-Indian Empire had not only reached its natural limits but it had trampled out the last vestiges of independent Indian states. All warlike native tribes were subdued, all serious internal conflicts were at an end, and the late incorporation of Oudh[26] proved satisfactorily that the remnants of the so-called independent Indian principalities exist on sufferance only. Hence a great change in the position of the East India Company. It no longer attacked one part of India by the help of another part, but found itself placed at the head, and the whole of India at its feet. No longer conquering, it had become *the* conqueror. The armies at its disposition no longer had to extend its dominion, but only to maintain it. From soldiers they were converted into policemen; 200,000,000 natives being curbed by a native army of 200,000 men, officered by Englishmen, and that native army, in its turn, being kept in check by an English army numbering 40,000 only. On first view, it is evident that the allegiance of the Indian people rests on the fidelity of the native army, in creating which the British rule simultaneously organized the first general centre of resistance which the Indian people was ever possessed of. How far that native army may be relied upon is clearly shown by its recent

2*

mutinies, breaking out as soon as the war with Persia[27] had almost denuded the Presidency of Bengal of its European soldiers. Before this there had been mutinies in the Indian army, but the present revolt[28] is distinguished by characteristic and fatal features. It is the first time that sepoy regiments have murdered their European officers; that Mussulmans and Hindus, renouncing their mutual antipathies, have combined against their common masters; that "disturbances beginning with the Hindus, have actually ended in placing on the throne of Delhi a Mohammedan Emperor";* that the mutiny has not been confined to a few localities; and lastly, that the revolt in the Anglo-Indian army has coincided with a general disaffection exhibited against English supremacy on the part of the great Asiatic nations, the revolt of the Bengal army being, beyond doubt, intimately connected with the Persian and Chinese wars.[29]

The alleged cause of the dissatisfaction which began to spread four months ago in the Bengal army was the apprehension on the part of the natives lest the Government should interfere with their religion. The serving out of cartridges, the paper of which was said to have been greased with the fat of bullocks and pigs, and the compulsory biting of which was, therefore, considered by the natives as an infringement of their religious prescriptions, gave the signal for local disturbances. On the 22d of January an incendiary fire broke out in cantonments a short distance from Calcutta. On the 25th of February the 19th Native Regiment mutinied at Berhampore, the men objecting to the cartridges served out to them. On the 31st of March that regiment was disbanded; at the end of March the 34th Sepoy Regiment, stationed at Barrackpore, allowed one of its men to advance with a loaded musket upon the parade-ground in front of the line, and, after having called his comrades to mutiny, he was permitted to attack and wound the Adjutant and Sergeant-Major of his regiment. During the hand-to-hand conflict, that ensued, hundreds of sepoys looked passively on, while others participated in the struggle, and attacked the officers with the butt ends of their muskets. Subsequently that regiment was also disbanded. The month of April was signalized by incendiary fires in several cantonments of the Bengal army at Allahabad, Agra, Ambala, by a mutiny of the 3d Regiment of Light Cavalry at Meerut, and by similar appearances of disaffection in the Madras and Bombay armies. At the beginning of May an

---

* Bahadur Shah II. —*Ed.*

émeute was preparing at Lucknow, the capital of Oudh, which was, however, prevented by the promptitude of Sir H. Lawrence. On the 9th of May the mutineers of the 3d Light Cavalry of Meerut were marched off to jail, to undergo the various terms of imprisonment to which they were sentenced. On the evening of the following day the troopers of the 3d Cavalry, together with the two native regiments, the 11th and 20th, assembled upon the parade-ground, killed the officers endeavouring to pacify them, set fire to the cantonments, and slew all the Englishmen they were able to lay hands on. Although the British part of the brigade mustered a regiment of infantry, another of cavalry, and an overwhelming force of horse and foot artillery, they were not able to move until nightfall. Having inflicted but little harm on the mutineers, they allowed them to betake themselves to the open field and to throw themselves into Delhi, some forty miles distant from Meerut. There they were joined by the native garrison, consisting of the 38th, 54th and 74th regiments of infantry, and a company of native artillery. The British officers were attacked, all Englishmen within reach of the rebels were murdered, and the heir* of the late Mogul** of Delhi proclaimed King of India. Of the troops sent to the rescue of Meerut, where order had been re-established, six companies of native sappers and miners, who arrived on the 15th of May, murdered their commanding officer, Major Frazer, and made at once for the open country, pursued by troops of horse artillery and several of the 6th Dragoon Guards. Fifty or sixty of the mutineers were shot, but the rest contrived to escape to Delhi. At Ferozepore, in the Punjab, the 57th and 45th Native Infantry regiments mutinied, but were put down by force. Private letters from Lahore state the whole of the native troops to be in an undisguised state of mutiny. On the 19th of May, unsuccessful efforts were made by the sepoys stationed at Calcutta to get possession of Fort St. William.[30] Three regiments arrived from Bushire at Bombay were at once dispatched to Calcutta.

In reviewing these events, one is startled by the conduct of the British commander***at Meerut—his late appearance on the field of battle being still less incomprehensible than the weak manner in which he pursued the mutineers. As Delhi is situated on the right and Meerut on the left bank of the Jumna—the two banks being joined at Delhi by one bridge only—nothing

* Bahadur Shah II.—*Ed.*

** Akbar II.—*Ed.*

*** General Hewitt.—*Ed.*

could have been easier than to cut off the retreat of the fugitives.

Meanwhile, martial law has been proclaimed in all the disaffected districts; forces, consisting of natives mainly, are concentrating against Delhi from the north, the east and the south; the neighbouring princes are said to have pronounced for the English; letters have been sent to Ceylon to stop Lord Elgin and Gen. Ashburnham's forces, on their way to China; and finally, 14,000 British troops were to be dispatched from England to India in about a fortnight. Whatever obstacles the climate of India at the present season, and the total want of means of transportation, may oppose to the movements of the British forces, the rebels at Delhi are very likely to succumb without any prolonged resistance. Yet, even then, it is only the prologue of a most terrible tragedy that will have to be enacted.

Written by K. Marx on June 30, 1857.
Published in the *New-York Daily Tribune*, No. 5065, of July 15, 1857, as a leading article.

Printed according to the newspaper text

K. Marx

THE REVOLT IN INDIA

London, July 17, 1857

On the 8th of June, just a month had passed since Delhi fell into the hands of the revolted sepoys and the proclamation by them of a Mogul Emperor.* Any notion, however, of the mutineers being able to keep the ancient capital of India against the British forces would be preposterous. Delhi is fortified only by a wall and a simple ditch, while the heights surrounding and commanding it are already in the possession of the English, who, even without battering the walls, might enforce its surrender in a very short period by the easy process of cutting off its supply of water. Moreover, a motley crew of mutineering soldiers who have murdered their own officers, torn asunder the ties of discipline, and not succeeded in discovering a man upon whom to bestow the supreme command, are certainly the body least likely to organize a serious and protracted resistance. To make confusion more confused, the checkered Delhi ranks are daily swelling from the fresh arrivals of new contingents of mutineers from all parts of the Bengal Presidency, who, as if on a preconcerted plan, are throwing themselves into the doomed city. The two sallies which, on the 30th and 31st of May, the mutineers risked without the walls, and in both of which they were repulsed with heavy losses, seem to have proceeded from despair rather than from any feeling of self-reliance or strength. The only thing to be wondered at is the slowness of the British operations, which, to some degree, however, may be accounted for by the horrors of the season and the want of means of transport. Apart from Gen. Anson, the commander-in-chief, French letters state that about 4,000 European troops have already fallen victims of the deathly heat, and even the English

* Bahadur Shah II. —*Ed.*

papers confess that in the engagements before Delhi the men suffered more from the sun than from the shot of the enemy. In consequence of its scanty means of conveyance, the main British force stationed at Ambala consumed about twenty-seven days in its march upon Delhi, so that it moved at the rate of about one and a half hours per day. A further delay was caused by the absence of heavy artillery at Ambala, and the consequent necessity of bringing over a siegetrain from the nearest arsenal, which was as far off as Phillaur, on the further side of the Sutlej.

With all that, the news of the fall of Delhi may be daily expected; but what next? If the uncontested possession by the rebels during a month of the traditionary centre of the Indian Empire acted perhaps as the most powerful ferment in completely breaking up the Bengal army, in spreading mutiny and desertion from Calcutta to the Punjab in the north, and to Rajputana in the west, and i shaking the British authority from one end of India to the other, no greater mistake could be committed than to suppose that the fall of Delhi, though it may throw consternation among the ranks of the sepoys, should suffice either to quench the rebellion, to stop its progress, or to restore the British rule. Of the whole native Bengal army, mustering about 80,000 men—composed of about 28,000 Rajputs, 23,000 Brahmins, 13,000 Mohammedans, 5,000 Hindus of inferior castes, and the rest Europeans—30,000 have disappeared in consequence of mutiny, desertion, or dismission from the ranks. As to the rest of that army, several of the regiments have openly declared that they will remain faithful and support the British authority, excepting in the matter in which the native troops are now engaged: they will not aid the authorities against the mutineers of the native regiments, and will, on the contrary, assist their "bhaies" (brothers). The truth of this has been exemplified in almost every station from Calcutta. The native regiments remained passive for a time; but, as soon as they fancied themselves strong enough, they mutinied. An Indian correspondent of the London *Times*[31] leaves no doubt as to the "loyalty" of the regiments which have not yet pronounced, and the native inhabitants who have not yet made common cause with the rebels.

"If you read," he says "that *all is quiet*, understand it to mean that the native troops have not yet risen in open mutiny; that the discontented part of the inhabitants are not yet in open rebellion; that they are either too weak, or fancy themselves to be so, or that they are waiting for a more fitting time. Where you read of the 'manifestation of loyalty' in any of the Bengal native regiments, cavalry or infantry, understand it to mean that one-half of the regiments thus favourably mentioned only are really faithful; the other half are but acting a part, the better to find the Europeans off their guard, when the proper time arrives, or, by warding off suspicion, have it the more in their power to aid their mutinous companions."

In the Punjab, open rebellion has only been prevented by disbanding the native troops. In Oudh, the English can only be said to keep Lucknow, the residency, while everywhere else the native regiments have revolted, escaped with their ammunition, burned all the bungalows to the ground, and joined with the inhabitants who have taken up arms. Now, the real position of the English army is best demonstrated by the fact that it was thought necessary, in the Punjab as well as the Rajputana, to establish flying corps. This means that the English cannot depend either on their sepoy troops or on the natives to keep the communication open between their scattered forces. Like the French during the Peninsular war,[32] they command only the spot of ground held by their own troops, and the next neighbourhood domineered by that spot; while for communication between the disjoined members of their army they depend on flying corps, the action of which, most precarious in itself, loses naturally in intensity in the same measure that it spreads over a greater extent of space. The actual insufficiency of the British forces is further proved by the fact that, for removing treasures from disaffected stations, they were constrained to have them conveyed by sepoys themselves, who, without any exception, broke out in rebellion on the march, and absconded with the treasures confided to them. As the troops sent from England will, in the best case, not arrive before November, and as it would be still more dangerous to draw off European troops from the presidencies of Madras and Bombay—the 10th Regiment of Madras sepoys, having already shown symptoms of disaffection—any idea of collecting the regular taxes throughout the Bengal Presidency must be abandoned, and the process of decomposition be allowed to go on. Even if we suppose that the Burmese will not improve the occasion, that the Maharajah of Gwalior* will continue supporting the English, and the Ruler of Nepal,** commanding the finest Indian army, remain quiet; that disaffected Peshawar will not combine with the restless hill tribes, and that the Shah of Persia*** will not be silly enough

* Sindhia. —*Ed.*

** Jang Bahadur. —*Ed.*

*** Nasr-ed-Din. —*Ed.*

to evacuate Herat — still, the whole Bengal Presidency must be reconquered, and the whole Anglo-Indian army remade. The cost of this enormous enterprise will altogether fall upon the British people. As to the notion put forward by Lord Granville in the House of Lords, of the East India Company being able to raise, by Indian loans, the necessary means, its soundness may be judged from the effects produced by the disturbed state of the north-western provinces on the Bombay money market. An immediate panic seized the native capitalists, very large sums were withdrawn from the banks, government securities proved almost unsaleable, and hoarding to a great extent commenced not only in Bombay but in its environs also.

Written by K. Marx on July 17, 1857.
Published in the *New-York Daily Tribune*, No 5082, of August 4, 1857.

Printed according to the newspaper text

K. Marx

THE INDIAN QUESTION

London, July 28, 1857

The three hours' speech delivered last night in "The Dead House",[33] by Mr. Disraeli, will gain rather than lose by being read instead of being listened to. For some time, Mr. Disraeli affects an awful solemnity of speech, an elaborate slowness of utterance and a passionless method of formality, which, however consistent they may be with his peculiar notions of the dignity becoming a Minister in expectance, are really distressing to his tortured audience. Once he succeeded in giving even commonplaces the pointed appearance of epigrams. Now he contrives to bury even epigrams in the conventional dullness of respectability. An orator who, like Mr. Disraeli, excels in handling the dagger rather than in wielding the sword, should have been the last to forget Voltaire's warning, that "*Tous les genres sont bons excepté le genre ennuyeux.*"*

Besides these technical peculiarities which characterize Mr. Disraeli's present manner of eloquence, he, since Palmerston's accession to power, has taken good care to deprive his parliamentary exhibitions of every possible interest of actuality. His speeches are not intended to carry his motions, but his motions are intended to prepare for his speeches. They might be called self-denying motions, since they are so constructed as neither to harm the adversary, if carried, nor to damage the proposer, if lost. They mean, in fact, to be neither carried nor lost, but simply to be dropped. They belong neither to the acids nor to the alkalis, but are born neutrals. The speech is not the vehicle of action, but the hypocrisy of action affords the

* "All styles are good save the tiresome kind." Voltaire. Preface to the comedy *L'enfant prodigue*. —*Ed.*

opportunity for a speech. Such, indeed, may be the classical and final form of parliamentary eloquence; but then, at all events, the final form of parliamentary eloquence must not demur to sharing the fate of all final forms of parliamentarism —that of being ranged under the category of nuisances. Action, as Aristotle said, is the ruling law of the drama.* So it is of political oratory. Mr. Disraeli's speech on the Indian revolt might be published in the tracts of the Society for the Propagation of Useful Knowledge, or it might be delivered to a mechanics' institution, or tendered as a prize essay to the Academy of Berlin. This curious impartiality of his speech as to the place where, and the time when, and the occasion on which it was delivered, goes far to prove that it fitted neither place, time, nor occasion. A chapter on the decline of the Roman Empire which might read exceedingly well in Montesquieu or Gibbon[34] would prove an enormous blunder if put in the mouth of a Roman Senator, whose peculiar business it was to stop that very decline. It is true that in our modern parliaments, a part lacking neither dignity nor interest might be imagined of an independent orator who, while despairing of influencing the actual course of events, should content himself to assume a position of ironical neutrality. Such a part was more or less successfully played by the late M. Garnier-Pagés —not the Garnier-Pagés of Provisional Government memory in Louis Philippe's Chamber of Deputies; but Mr. Disraeli, the avowed leader of an obsolete faction,[35] would consider even success in this line as a supreme failure. The revolt of the Indian army afforded certainly a magnificent opportunity for oratorical display. But, apart from his dreary manner of treating the subject, what was the gist of the motion which he made the pretext for his speech? It was no motion at all. He feigned to be anxious for becoming acquainted with two official papers, the one of which he was not quite sure to exist, and the other of which he was sure not immediately to bear on the subject in question. Consequently his speech and his motion lacked any point of contact save this, that the motion heralded a speech without an object, and that the object confessed itself not worth a speech. Still, as the highly elaborated opinion of the most distinguished out-of-office statesman of England, Mr. Disraeli's speech ought to attract the attention of foreign countries. I shall content myself with giving in his *ipsissima verba* a short analysis

* Aristotle, *Poetics*, Chap. VI. —*Ed.*

of his "considerations on the decline of the Anglo-Indian Empire".

"Does the disturbance in India indicate a military mutiny, or is it a national revolt? Is the conduct of the troops the consequence of a sudden impulse, or is it the result of an organised conspiracy?"

Upon these points Mr. Disraeli asserts the whole question to hinge. Until the last ten years, he affirmed, the British Empire in India was founded on the old principle of *divide et impera* —but that principle was put into action by respecting the different nationalities of which India consisted, by avoiding to tamper with their religion, and by protecting their landed property. The sepoy army served as a safety-valve to absorb the turbulent spirits of the country. But of late years a new principle has been adopted in the government of India —the principle of destroying nationality. The principle has been realized by the forcible destruction of native princes, the disturbance of the settlement of property, and the tampering with the religion of the people. In 1848 the financial difficulties of the East India Company had reached that point that it became necessary to augment its revenues one way or the other. Then a minute in Council was published,[36] in which was laid down the principle, almost without disguise, that the only mode by which an increased revenue could be obtained was by enlarging the British territories at the expense of the native princes. Accordingly, on the death of the Rajah of Satara,* his adoptive heir was not acknowledged by the East India Company, but the Raj absorbed in its own dominions. From that moment the system of annexation was acted upon whenever a native prince died without natural heirs. The principle of adoption —the very cornerstone of Indian society — was systematically set aside by the Government. Thus were forcibly annexed to the British Empire the Rajs of more than a dozen independent princes from 1848-54. In 1854 the Raj of Berar, which comprised 80,000 square miles of land, a population from 4,000,000 to 5,000,000, and enormous treasures, was forcibly seized. Mr. Disraeli ends the list of forcible annexations with Oudh, which brought the East Indian Government in collision not only with the Hindus, but also with the Mohammedans. Mr. Disraeli then goes on showing how the settlement of property in India was disturbed by the new system of government during the last ten years.

* Appa Sahib. — *Ed.*

"The principle of the law of adoption," he says, "is not the prerogative of princes and principalities in India, it applies to every man in Hindustan who has landed property, and who professes the Hindu religion."

I quote a passage:

"The great feudatory, or jagheerdar, who holds his lands by public service to his lord; and the enamdar, who holds his land free of all land-tax, who corresponds, if not precisely, in a popular sense, at least, with our freeholder — both of these classes — classes most numerous in India — always, on the failure of their natural heirs, find in this principle the means of obtaining successors to their estates. Those classes were all touched by the annexation of Satara, they were touched by the annexation of the territories of the ten inferior but independent princes to whom I have already alluded, and they were more than touched, they were terrified to the last degree, when the annexation of the Raj of Berar took place. What man was safe? What feudatory, what freeholder who had not a child of his own loins was safe throughout India? (Hear, hear.) These were not idle fears; they were extensively acted upon and reduced to practice. The resumption of jagheers and of inams commenced for the first time in India. There have been, no doubt, impolitic moments when attempts have been made to inquire into titles, but no one had ever dreamt of abolishing the law of adoption; therefore, no authority, no Government had ever been in a position to resume jagheers and inams the holders of which had left no natural heirs. Here was a new source of revenue; but while all these things were acting upon the minds of these classes of Hindus, the Government took another step to disturb the settlement of property, to which I must now call the attention of the House. The House is aware, no doubt, from reading the evidence taken before the Committee of 1853, that there are great portions of the land of India which are exempt from the land-tax. Being free from land-tax in India is far more than equivalent to freedom from the land-tax in this country, for speaking generally and popularly, the land-tax in India is the whole taxation of the state.

"The origin of these grants is difficult to penetrate, but they are undoubtedly of great antiquity. They are of different kinds. Besides the private freeholds, which are very extensive, there are large grants of land free from the land-tax with which mosques and temples have been endowed."

On the pretext of fraudulent claims of exemption, the British Governor-General* took upon himself to examine the titles of the Indian landed estates. Under the new system, established in 1848,

"That plan of investigating titles was at once embraced, as a proof of a powerful Government, a vigorous Executive, and most fruitful source of public revenue. Therefore commissions were issued to inquire into titles to landed estates in the Presidency of Bengal and adjoining country. They were also issued in the Presidency of Bombay, and surveys were ordered to be made in the newly-settled provinces, in order that these commissions might be conducted, when the surveys were completed, with due efficiency. Now there is no doubt that, during the last nine years, the action of these commissions of inquiry into the freehold property of landed estates in India has been going on at an enormous rate, and immense results have been obtained."

* Dalhousie. —*Ed.*

Mr. Disraeli computes that the resumption of estates from their proprietors is not less than £500,000 a year in the Presidency of Bengal; £370,000 in the Presidency of Bombay; £200,000 in the Punjab, etc. Not content with this one method of seizing upon the property of the natives, the British Government discontinued the pensions to the native grandees, to pay which it was bound by treaty.

"This," says Mr. Disraeli, "is confiscation by a new means, but upon a most extensive, startling and shocking scale."

Mr. Disraeli then treats the tampering with the religion of the natives, a point upon which we need not dwell. From all his premises he arrives at the conclusion that the present Indian disturbance is not a military mutiny, but a national revolt, of which the sepoys are the acting instruments only. He ends his harangue by advising the Government to turn their attention to the internal improvement of India, instead of pursuing its present course of aggression.

Written by K. Marx on July 28, 1857. Published in the *New-York Daily Tribune*, No. 5091, of August 14, 1857.

Printed according to the newspaper text

K. Marx

DISPATCHES FROM INDIA[37]

London, July 31, 1857

The last Indian mail, conveying news from Delhi up to the 17th June, and from Bombay up to the 1st of July, realizes the most gloomy anticipations. When Mr. Vernon Smith, the President of the Board of Control,[38] first informed the House of Commons of the Indian revolt, he confidently stated that the next mail would bring the news that Delhi had been razed to the ground. The mail arrived, but Delhi was not yet "wiped out of the pages of history". It was then said that the battery train could not be brought up before the 9th of June, and that the attack on the doomed city must consequently be delayed to that date. The 9th of June passed away without being distinguished by any remarkable incident. On the 12th and 15th June some events occurred, but rather in the opposite direction, Delhi being not stormed by the English, but the English being attacked by the insurgents, the repeated sorties of whom were, however, repulsed. The fall of Delhi is thus again postponed, the alleged cause being now no longer the sole want of siege-artillery, but General Barnard's resolution to wait upon reinforcements, as his forces — about 3,000 men — were totally inadequate to the capture of the ancient capital defended by 30,000 sepoys, and possessed of all the military stores. The rebels had even established a camp outside the Ajmer gate. Until now, all military writers were unanimous in considering an English force of 3,000 men quite sufficient for crushing a sepoy army of 30,000 or 40,000 men; and if such was not the case, how could England — to use an expression of the London *Times* — ever be able to "reconquer" India?

The British army in India amounts actually to 30,000 men. The utmost number they can dispatch from England within the next half year cannot exceed 20,000 or 25,000 men, of whom

6,000 men are to fill up vacancies among the European ranks in India, and of whom the additional force of 18,000 or 19,000 men will be reduced by loss from the voyage, by loss from the climate, and by other casualties to about 14,000 troops able to appear on the theatre of war. The British army must resolve upon meeting the mutineers in very disproportionate numbers, or it must renounce meeting them at all. Still we are at a loss to understand the slowness of the concentration of their forces around Delhi. If at this season of the year, the heat proves an invincible obstacle, which it did not in the days of Sir Charles Napier, some months later, on the arrival of the European troops, the rains will afford a still more conclusive pretext for a standstill. It should never be forgotten that the present mutiny had, in fact, already begun in the month of January, and that the British Government had thus received ample warning for keeping its powder dry and its forces ready.

The prolonged hold of Delhi by the sepoys in face of an English besieging army has, of course, produced its natural result. The mutiny was spreading to the very gates of Calcutta, fifty Bengal regiments had ceased to exist, the Bengal army itself had become a myth of the past, and the Europeans, dispersed over an immense extent of land, and brocked up in insulated spots, were either butchered by the rebels, or had taken up position of desperate defence. At Calcutta itself the Christian inhabitants formed a volunteer guard, after a plot, said to have been most complete in its details, for surprising the seat of the Government, had been discovered, and the native troops there stationed had been disbanded. At Benares, an attempt at disarming a native regiment was resisted by a body of Sikhs and the 13th Irregular Cavalry. This fact is very important, as it shows that the Sikhs, like the Mohammedans, were making common cause with the Brahmins, and that thus a general union against the British rule, of all the different tribes, was rapidly progressing. It had been an article of faith with the English people, that the sepoy army constituted their whole strength in India. Now, all at once, they feel quite satisfied that that very army constitutes their sole danger. During the last Indian debates, Mr. Vernon Smith, the President of the Board of Control, still declared that "the fact cannot be too much insisted upon that there is no connection whatever between the native princes and the revolt". Two days later the same Vernon Smith had to publish a dispatch containing this ominous paragraph:

"On the 14th of June the ex-King of Oudh,* implicated in the conspiracy by intercepted papers, was lodged in Fort William, and his followers disarmed."

By and by there will ooze out other facts able to convince even John Bull himself that what he considers a military mutiny is in truth a national revolt.

The English press feigns to derive great comfort from the conviction that the revolt had not yet spread beyond the boundaries of the Bengal Presidency, and that not the least doubt was entertained of the loyalty of the Bombay and Madras armies. However, this pleasant view of the case seems singularly to clash with the fact conveyed by the last mail of a mutiny of the Nizam's ** cavalry having broken out at Aurangabad. Aurangabad being the capital of the district of the same name which belongs to the Bombay Presidency, the truth is that the last mail announces a commencement of revolt of the Bombay army. The Aurangabad mutiny is, indeed, said to have been at once put down by General Woodburn. But was not the Meerut mutiny said to have been put down at once? Did not the Lucknow mutiny, after having been quenched by Sir H. Lawrence, make a more formidable reappearance a fortnight later? Will it not be recollected that the very first announcement of mutiny in the Indian army was accompanied with the announcement of restored order? Although the bulk of the Bombay and Madras armies is composed of low caste men, there are still mixed to every regiment some hundred Rajputs, a number quite sufficient to form the collecting links with the high-caste rebels of the Bengal army. The Punjab is declared to be quiet, but at the same time we are informed that "at Ferozepore, on the 13th of June, military executions had taken place"; while Vaughan's corps—5th Punjab Infantry—is praised for "having behaved admirably in pursuit of the 55th Native Infantry". This, it must be confessed, is a very queer sort of quiet.

Written by K. Marx on July 31, 1857. Published in the *New-York Daily Tribune*, No. 5091, of August 14, 1857.

Printed according to the newspaper text

* Wajid Ali Shah.—*Ed.*

** Sovereign of Hyderabad Principality.—*Ed.*

K. Marx

STATE OF THE INDIAN INSURRECTION

London, August 4, 1857

On the arrival at London of the voluminous reports conveyed by the last Indian mail, the meagre outlines of which had been anticipated by the electric telegraph, the rumour of the capture of Delhi was rapidly spreading and winning so much consistency as to influence the transactions of the Stock Exchange. It was another edition of the capture of Sevastopol hoax,[39] on a reduced scale. The slightest examination of the dates and contents of the Madras papers, from which the favourable news was avowedly derived, would have sufficed to dispel the delusion. The Madras information professed to rest upon private letters from Agra dated June 17, but an official notification, issued at Lahore, on the 17th of June, announces that up to 4 o'clock in the afternoon of the 16th, all was quiet before Delhi, while *The Bombay Times*,[40] dated July 1, states that "General Barnard was waiting for reinforcements on the morning of the 17th, after having repelled several sorties". This much, as to the date of the Madras information. As to its contents, these are evidently made up of General Barnard's bulletin, dated June 8, on his forcible occupation of the heights of Delhi, and of some private reports relating to the sallies of the besieged on the 12th and 14th June.

A military plan of Delhi and its cantonments has at last been compiled by Captain Lawrence, from the unpublished plans of the East India Company. Hence we see that Delhi is not quite so weakly fortified as was at first asserted, nor quite so strongly as is now pretended. It possesses a citadel, to be taken by escalade or by regular approaches. The walls, being more than seven miles in extent, are built of solid masonry, but of no great height. The ditch is narrow and not very deep, and the flanking works do not properly enfilade the curtain. Martello towers exist at intervals. They are semicircular in form, and loopholed for musketry. Spiral staircases lead from the top of the walls down through the towers to chambers, on a level with the ditch, and those are loopholed for infantry fire, which may prove very annoying to an escalading party crossing the ditch. The bastions defending the curtains are also furnished with banquettes for riflemen, but these may be kept down by shelling. When the insurrection broke out, the arsenal in the interior of the city contained 900,000 cartridges, two complete siegetrains, a large number of field guns and 10,000 muskets. The powder-magazine had been long since removed, at the desire of the inhabitants, from the city to the cantonments outside Delhi, and contained not less than 10,000 barrels. The commanding heights occupied by Gen. Barnard on the 8th of June are situated in a north-westerly direction from Delhi, where the cantonments outside the walls were also established.

From the description, resting on authentic plans, it will be understood that the stronghold of the revolt must have succumbed before a single *coup de main*, if the British force now before Delhi had been there on the 26th of May, and they could have been there if supplied with sufficient carriage. A review of the list published in *The Bombay Times*, and republished in the London papers, of the number of regiments that had revolted, to the end of June, and of the dates on which they revolted, proves conclusively that, on the 26th of May, Delhi was yet occupied by 4,000 to 5,000 men only; a force which could not one moment have thought of defending a wall seven miles in extent. Meerut being only forty miles distant from Delhi, and having, since the commencement of 1853, always served as the headquarters of the Bengal artillery, possessed the principal laboratory for military scientific purposes, and afforded the parade-ground for exercise in the use of field and siege ordnance; it becomes the more incomprehensible that the British commander was in want of the means necessary for the execution of one of those *coups de main* by which the British forces in India always know how to secure their supremacy over the natives. First we were informed that the siege-train* was waited for; then that reinforcements were wanted; and now *The Press*,[41] one of the best informed London papers, tells us,

---

* See this collection, p. 53. —*Ed.*

"It is known by our Government for a fact that General Barnard is deficient in stores and ammunition, and that his supply of the latter is limited to 24 rounds a man."

From General Barnard's own bulletin on the occupation of the heights of Delhi, which is dated the 8th of June, we see that he originally intended assailing Delhi on the following day. Instead of being able to follow up this plan, he was, by one accident or the other, confined to taking up the defensive against the besieged.

At this very moment it is extremely difficult to compute the forces on either part. The statements of the Indian press are altogether self-contradictory; but we think some reliance may be put upon an Indian correspondence of the Bonapartist *Pays*,[42] which seems to emanate from the French Consul at Calcutta. According to his statement, the army of Gen. Barnard was, on the 14th of June, composed of about 5,700 men, which was expected to be doubled (?) by the reinforcements expected on the 20th of the same month. His train was composed of 30 heavy siege guns, while the forces of the insurgents were estimated at 40,000 men, badly organized, but richly furnished with all the means of attack and defence.

We remark *en passant*, that the 3,000 insurgents encamped without the Ajmer gate, probably in the Ghazi Khan's tombs, are not, as some London papers imagine, fronting the English force, but, on the contrary, separated from them by the whole breadth of Delhi; the Ajmer gate being situated on one extremity of the south-western part of modern Delhi to the north of the ruins of ancient Delhi. On that side of the town nothing can prevent the insurgents from establishing some more such camps. On the north-eastern, or river side of the city, they command the ship bridge, and remain in continued connection with their countrymen, able to receive uninterrupted supplies of men and stores. On a smaller scale Delhi offers the image of a fortress, keeping (like Sevastopol) open its lines of communication with the interior of its own country.

The delay in the British operations has not only allowed the besieged to concentrate large numbers for the defence, but the sentiment of having held Delhi during many weeks, harassed the European forces through repeated sallies, together with the news daily pouring in of fresh revolts of the entire army, has, of course, strengthened the *morale* of the sepoys. The English, with their small forces, can, of course, not think of investing the town, but must storm it. However, if the next regular mail bring not the news of the capture of Delhi, we may almost be sure that, for some months, all serious operations on the part of the British will have to be suspended. The rainy season will have set in in real earnest, and protect the north-eastern face of the city by filling the ditch with "the deep and rapid current of the Jumna", while a thermometer ranging from 75 to 102° , combined with an average fall of nine inches of rain, would scourge the Europeans with the genuine Asiatic cholera. Then would be verified the words of Lord Ellenborough,

> "I am of opinion that Sir H. Barnard cannot remain where he is — the climate forbids it. When the heavy rains set in he will be cut off from Meerut, from Ambala and from the Punjab; he will be imprisoned in a very narrow strip of land, and he will be in a situation, I will not say of peril, but in a situation which can only end in ruin and destruction. I trust that he will retire in time."

Everything, then, as far as Delhi is concerned, depends on the question whether or not Gen. Barnard found himself sufficiently provided with men and ammunition to undertake the assault of Delhi during the last weeks of June. On the other hand, a retreat on his part would immensely strengthen the moral force of the insurrection, and perhaps decide the Bombay and Madras armies upon openly joining it.

Written by K. Marx on August 4, 1857. Published in the *New-York Daily Tribune*, No. 5094, of August 18, 1857.

Printed according to the newspaper text

K. Marx

THE INDIAN INSURRECTION

London, August 14, 1857

When the Indian news, conveyed by the Trieste telegraph on the 30th of July, and by the Indian mail on the 1st of August,* first arrived, we showed at once, from their contents and their dates, that the capture of Delhi was a miserable hoax, and a very inferior imitation of the never-to-be-forgotten fall of Sevastopol. Yet such is the unfathomable depth of John Bull's gullibility, that his ministers, his stock-jobbers and his press had, in fact, contrived to persuade him that the very news which laid bare General Barnard's merely defensive position, contained evidence of the complete extermination of his enemies. From day to day this hallucination grew stronger, till it assumed at last such consistency as to induce even a veteran hand at similar matters, General Sir De Lacy Evans, to proclaim on the night of the 12th of August, amid the cheering echoes of the House of Commons, his belief in the truth of the rumour of the capture of Delhi. After this ridiculous exhibition, however, the bubble was ripe for bursting, and the following day, the 13th of August, brought successive telegraphic dispatches from Trieste and Marseilles, anticipating the Indian mails, and leaving no doubt as to the fact that on the 27th of June Delhi still stood where it had stood before, and that General Barnard, still confined to the defensive, but harassed by frequent furious sorties of the besieged, was very glad to have been able to hold his ground to that time.

In our opinion the next mail is likely to impart the news of the

* The reference is to a false report on the capture of Delhi (see this collection, p. 51). —*Ed.*

retreat of the English army, or at least facts foreshadowing such a retrograde movement. It is certain that the extent of the walls of Delhi forbids the belief that the whole of them can be effectively manned, and, on the contrary, invites the *coups de main* to be executed by concentration and surprise. But Gen. Barnard seems imbued with European notions of fortified towns and sieges and bombardments, rather than prone to those bold eccentricities by which Sir Charles Napier knew how to thunderstrike Asiatic minds. His forces are, indeed, said to have been increased to about 12,000 men, 7,000 Europeans and 5,000 "faithful natives"; but on the other hand, it is not denied that the rebels were daily receiving new reinforcements, so that we may fairly assume that the numerical disproportion between besiegers and besieged has remained the same. Moreover, the only point by the surprise of which General Barnard might insure certain success is the Mogul's Palace, which occupies a commanding position, but the access to which from the riverside must become impracticable from the effect of the rainy season, which will have set in, while an attack on the palace between the Cashmere gate and the river would inflict on the assailants the greatest risk in case of failure. Finally, the setting in of the rains is sure to make the securing of his line of communication and retreat the principal object of the General's operations. In one word, we see no reason to believe that he, with his still inadequate forces, should venture upon risking, at the most impracticable period of the year, what he shrunk from undertaking at a more seasonable time. That in spite of the judicial blindness by which the London press contrives to fool itself, there are entertained serious misgivings in the highest quarters, may be seen from Lord Palmerston's organ, *The Morning Post*.[43] The venal gentleman of that paper informs us:

> "We doubt whether even by the next mail after this, we shall hear of the capture of Delhi; *but* we do expect that, as *soon* as the troops now on their march to join the besiegers shall have arrived, with a *sufficiency of large guns*, which it seems are still missing, we shall receive intelligence of the fall of the stronghold of the rebels."

It is evident that, by dint of weakness, vacillation, and direct blunders, the British generals have contrived to raise Delhi to the dignity of the political and military centre of the Indian revolt. A retreat of the English army, after a prolonged siege, or a mere staying on the defensive, will be regarded as a positive defeat, and give the signal to a general outbreak. It would moreover expose the British troops to a fearful mortality, from which till now they have been protected by the great excitement inherent to a siege full of sorties, encounters, and a hope of soon wreaking a bloody vengeance on their enemies. As to the talk about the apathy of the Hindus, or even their sympathy with British rule, it is all nonsense. The princes, like true Asiatics, are watching their opportunity. The people in the whole Presidency of Bengal, where not kept in check by a handful of Europeans, are enjoying a blessed anarchy; but there is nobody there against whom they could rise. It is a curious *quid pro quo* to expect an Indian revolt to assume the features of a European revolution.

In the presidencies of Madras and Bombay, the army having not yet pronounced, the people of course do not stir. The Punjab, at last, is to this moment the principal central station of the European forces, while its native army is disarmed. To rouse it, the neighbouring semi-independent princes must throw their weight into the scale. But that such a ramification of conspiracy as exhibited by the Bengal army could not have been carried on on such an immense scale without the secret connivance and support of the natives, seems as certain as that the great difficulties the English meet with in obtaining supplies and transports—the principal cause of the slow concentration of their troops—do not witness to the good feelings of the peasantry.

The other news conveyed by the telegraphic dispatches are so far important as they show us the revolt rising on the extreme confines of the Punjab, in Peshawar, and on the other hand striding in a southern direction from Delhi to the Presidency of Bombay, through the stations of Jhansi, Sagar, Indore, Mhow, till we arrive at last at Aurangabad, only 180 miles north-east of Bombay. With respect to Jhansi in Bundelkhand, we may remark that it is fortified and may thus become another centre of armed rebellion. On the other hand, it is stated that Gen. Van Cortlandt has defeated the mutineers at Sirsa, on his road from the north-west to join Gen. Barnard's force before Delhi, from which he was still 170 miles distant. He had to pass by Jhansi, where he would again encounter the rebels. As to the preparations made by the Home Government, Lord Palmerston seems to think that the most circuitous line is the shortest, and consequently sends his troops round the Cape, instead of through Egypt. The fact that some thousand men destined for China have been intercepted at Ceylon and directed to Calcutta, where the 5th Fusileers actually arrived on the 2nd of July, has afforded him the occasion for breaking a bad joke on those of his obedient Commons who still dared doubt that his Chinese war was quite a "windfall".

Written by K. Marx on August 14, 1857. Published in the *New-York Daily Tribune*, No. 5104, of August 29, 1857.

Printed according to the newspaper text

K. Marx

POLITICAL SITUATION IN EUROPE

The last sitting but one of the Commons before their prorogation was seized upon by Lord Palmerston to allow them to take some faint glimpses at the entertainments he keeps in store for the English public during the interregnum between the session that has passed away and the session that is to come. The first item of his programme is the announcement of the revival of the Persian war, which as he had stated some months ago was definitely terminated by a peace concluded on the 4th of March. General Sir De Lacy Evans having expressed the hope that Col. Jacob was ordered back to India with his forces now stationed on the Persian Gulf, Lord Palmerston stated plainly that until Persia had executed the engagements contracted by the treaty, Col. Jacob's troops could not be withdrawn. Herat, however, had not yet been evacuated. There were, on the contrary, rumours afloat affirming that additional forces had been sent by Persia to Herat. This, indeed, had been denied by the Persian Ambassador at Paris; but great doubts were justly entertained of the good faith of Persia, and consequently the British forces under Col. Jacob would continue to occupy Bushire. On the day following Lord Palmerston's statement, the news was conveyed by telegraphic dispatch of the categorical demand pressed upon the Persian Government by Mr. Murray for the evacuation of Herat — a demand which may be fairly considered the forerunner of a new declaration of war. Such is the first international effect of the Indian revolt.

The second item of Lord Palmerston's programme makes good for its want of details by the wide perspective it unrolls. When he first announced the withdrawal of large military forces from England to be dispatched to India, he answered his opponents, accusing them of denuding Great Britain of her defensive power, and thus affording foreign countries an opportunity to take advantage of her weakened position, that

> "the people of Great Britain would never tolerate any such proceeding, and that men would be raised suddenly and rapidly, sufficient for any contingency that would arrive."

Now, on the eve of the prorogation of Parliament, he speaks in quite a different strain. To the advice of Gen. De Lacy Evans to send out to India the troops in screw line of -battle ships, he did not reply, as he had done before, by asserting the superiority of the sail to the screw-propeller, but on the contrary, admitted that the General's plan appeared in the first instance highly advantageous. Yet, the House ought to bear in mind, that

> "there were other considerations, to be kept in view, in regard to the propriety of keeping up sufficient military and naval forces at home.... Certain circumstances pointed out the inexpediency of sending out of the country a greater naval force than was absolutely necessary. The steam line-of-battle ships were, no doubt, lying in ordinary, and were of no great use at present; but if any such events as had been alluded to took place, and they wanted their naval forces to put to sea, how could they meet *the danger which threatened*, if they allowed their line-of-battle ships to do the duty of transports to India? They should be falling into a grave error if they sent to India the fleet which *circumstances occurring in Europe* might render it necessary to arm *for their own defence at a very short notice*."

Lord Palmerston, it will not be denied, plants John Bull on the horns of a very fine dilemma. If he uses the adequate means for a decisive suppression of the Indian revolt, he will be attacked at home; and if he allows the Indian revolt to consolidate, he will, as Mr. Disraeli said, "find other characters on the stage, with whom to contend, besides the princes of India".

Before casting a glance at the "European circumstances" so mysteriously alluded to, it may not be amiss to gather up the confessions made during the same sitting of the Commons in regard to the actual position of the British forces in India. First, then, all sanguine hopes of a sudden capture of Delhi were dropped as if by mutual agreement, and the high-flying expectations of former days came down to the more rational view that they ought to congratulate themselves, if the English were able to maintain their posts until November, when the advance of the reinforcements sent from home was to take place. In the second instance, misgivings oozed out as to the probability of their losing the most important of those posts,

Cawnpore, on the fate of which, as Mr. Disraeli said, everything must depend, and the relief of which he considered of even greater import than the capture of Delhi. From its central position on the Ganges, its bearing on Oudh, Rohilkhand, Gwalior, and Bundelkhand, and its serving as an advanced fort to Delhi, Cawnpore is, in fact, in the present circumstances, a place of prime importance. Lastly, Sir F. Smith, one of the military members of the House, called its attention to the fact that, actually, there were no engineers and sappers with their Indian army, as all of them had deserted, and were likely "to make Delhi a second Saragossa."[44] On the other hand, Lord Palmerston had neglected to forward from England either any officers or men of the engineer corps.

Returning now to the European events said to be "looming in the future," we are at once astonished at the comment the London *Times* makes on Lord Palmerston's allusions. The French Constitution, it says, might be overthrown, or Napoleon disappear from the scene of life, and then there would be an end to the French alliance, upon which the present security rests. In other words, *The Times*, the great organ of the British Cabinet, while considering a revolution in France an event not unlikely to occur any day, simultaneously proclaims the present alliance to be founded not on the sympathies of the French people, but on mere conspiracy with the French usurper. Besides a revolution in France, there is the Danubian quarrel.[45] By the annulling of the Moldavian elections, it has not been made to subside, but only to enter on a new phase. There is, above all, the Scandinavian North, which, at a period not distant, is sure to become the theatre of great agitation, and, perhaps, may give the signal to an international conflict in Europe. Peace is still kept in the North, because two events are anxiously waited for —the death of the King of Sweden* and the abdication of his throne by the present King of Denmark. At a late meeting of naturalists at Christiania, the hereditary Prince of Sweden** declared emphatically in favour of a Scandinavian union. Being a man in the prime of life, of a resolute and energetic character, the Scandinavian party, mustering in its ranks the ardent youth of Sweden, Norway and Denmark, will consider his accession to the throne as the opportune moment

* Oscar I. —*Ed.*

** Charles Ludwig Eugen. —*Ed.*

for taking up arms. On the other hand, the weak and imbecile King of Denmark, Frederick VII, is said to have been at last allowed by the Countess Danner, his morganatic consort, to withdraw to private life, a permission hitherto refused him. It was on her account that Prince Ferdinand, the King's uncle, and the presumptive heir of the Danish throne, was induced to retire from state affairs, to which he afterward returned in consequence of an arrangement brought about by the other members of the royal family. Now, at this moment, the Countess Danner is said to be disposed to change her residence at Copenhagen for one at Paris, and even to prompt the King to bid farewell to the storms of political life by resigning his sceptre into the hands of Prince Ferdinand. This Prince Ferdinand, a man about 65 years of age, has always occupied the same position toward the Court of Copenhagen, which the Count of Artois—afterward Charles X—held toward the Court of the Tuileries. Obstinate, severe and ardent in his conservative faith, he has never condescended to feign adherence to the Constitutional system. Yet the first condition of his accession to the throne would be the acceptance on oath of a Constitution he openly detests. Hence the probability of international troubles, which the Scandinavian party, both in Sweden and Denmark, are firmly revolved upon turning to their own profit. On the other hand, the conflict between Denmark and the German duchies of Holstein and Schleswig,[46] supported in their claims by Prussia and Austria, would still more embroil matters, and entangle Germany in the agitations of the North; while the London treaty of 1852, guaranteeing the throne of Denmark to Prince Ferdinand, would involve Russia, France and England.

Written by K. Marx on August 21, 1857.
Published in the *New-York Daily Tribune*, No. 5110, of September 5, 1857, as a leading article.

Printed according to the newspaper text

K. Marx

*INVESTIGATION OF TORTURES IN INDIA[47]

Our London correspondent, whose letter with regard to the Indian revolt we published yesterday, very properly referred to some of the antecedents which prepared the way for this violent outbreak. We propose to-day to devote a moment to continuing that line of reflections, and to showing that the British rulers of India are by no means such mild and spotless benefactors of the Indian people as they would have the world believe. For this purpose, we shall resort to the official Blue Books[48] on the subject of East Indian torture, which were laid before the House of Commons during the sessions of 1856 and 1857. The evidence, it will be seen, is of a sort which cannot be gainsaid.

We have first the report of the Torture Commission at Madras,[49] which states its "belief in the general existence of torture for revenue purposes". It doubts whether

> "anything like an equal number of persons is annually subjected to violence on criminal charges, as for the fault of non-payment of revenue."

It declares that there was

> "one thing which had impressed the Commission even more painfully than the conviction that torture exists; it is the difficulty of obtaining redress which confronts the injured parties."

The reasons for this difficulty given by the Commissioners are: 1. The distances which those who wish to make complaints personally to the Collector have to travel involving expense and loss of time in attending upon his office; 2. The fear that applications by letter "will be returned with the ordinary indorsement of a reference to the tahsildar," the district police and revenue officer —that is, to the very man who, either in his person or through his petty police subordinates, has wronged him; 3. The inefficient means of procedure and punishment provided by law for officers of Government, even when formally accused or convicted of these practices. It seems that if a charge of this nature were proved before a magistrate, he could only punish by a fine of fifty rupees, or a month's imprisonment. The alternative consisted of handing over the accused

"to the criminal judge to be punished by him, or committed for trial before the Court of the Circuit."

The report adds that

"these seem to be tedious proceedings, applicable only to one class of offences, abuse of authority —namely, in police charges, and totally inadequate to the necessities of the case."

A police or revenue officer, who is the same person, as the revenue is collected by the police, when charged with extorting money, is first tried by the Assistant Collector; he then can appeal to the Collector; then to the Revenue Board. This Board may refer him to the Government or to the civil courts.

"In such a state of the law, no poverty-stricken ryot could contend against any wealthy revenue officer; and we are not aware of any complaints having been brought forward under these two regulations (of 1822 and 1828) by the people."

Further, this extorting of money applies only to taking the public money, or forcing a further contribution from the ryot for the officer to put into his own pocket. There is, therefore, no legal means of punishment whatever for the employment of force in collecting the public revenue.

The report from which these quotations are made applies only to the Presidency of Madras; but Lord Dalhousie himself, writing, in September, 1855, to the Directors,* says that

"he has long ceased to doubt that torture in one shape or other is practised by the lower subordinates in every British province."

The universal existence of torture as a financial institution of British India is thus officially admitted, but the admission is made in such a manner as to shield the British Government itself. In fact, the conclusion arrived at by the Madras Commission is that the practice of torture is entirely the fault of the lower Hindu officials, while the European servants of the

* Court of Directors of East India Company. —*Ed.*

Government had always, however unsuccessfully, done their best to prevent it. In answer to this assertion, the Madras Native Association presented, in January, 1856, a petition to Parliament, complaining of the torture investigation on the following grounds: 1. That there was scarcely any investigation at all, the Commission sitting only in the city of Madras, and for but three months, while it was impossible, except in very few cases, for the natives who had complaints to make to leave their homes; 2. That the Commissioners did not endeavour to trace the evil to its source; had they done so, it would have been discovered to be in the very system of collecting the revenue; 3. That no inquiry was made of the accused native officials as to what extent their superiors were acquainted with the practice.

> "The origin of this coercion," say the petitioners, "is not with the physical perpetrators of it, but descends to them from the officials immediately their superiors, which latter again are answerable for the estimated amount of the collection to their European superiors, these also being responsible on the same head to the highest authority of the Government."

Indeed, a few extracts from the evidence on which the Madras Report professes to be founded, will suffice to refute its assertion that "no blame is due to Englishmen". Thus, Mr. W. D. Kohlhoff, a merchant, says:

> "The modes of torture practised are various, and suitable to the fancy of the tahsildar or his subordinates, but whether any redress is received from higher authorities, it is difficult for me to tell, *as all complaints are generally referred to the tahsildars* for investigation and information."

Among the cases of complaint from natives, we find the following:

> "Last year, as our peasanum (principal paddy or rice crops) failed for want of rain, we were unable to pay as usual. When the jamabandi was made we claimed a remission on account of the losses, according to the terms of the agreement entered into in 1837, by us, when Mr. Eden was our collector. As this remission was not allowed, we refused to take our puttahs. The tahsildar then commenced to compel us to pay with great severity, from the month of June to August. I and others were placed in charge of persons who used to take us in the sun. There we were made to stoop and stones were put on our backs, and we were kept in the burning sand. After 8 o'clock, we were let to go to our rice. Such like ill treatment was continued during three months, during which we sometimes went to give our petitions to the collector, who refused to take them. We took these petitions and appealed to the Sessions Court, who transmitted them to the collector. Still we got no justice. In the month of September, a notice was served upon us, and twenty-five days after, our property was distrained, and afterward sold. Besides what I have mentioned, our women were also ill treated; the kittee was put upon their breasts."

A native Christian states in reply to questions put by the Commissioners:

"When a European or native regiment passes through, all the ryots are pressed to bring in provisions, etc., *for nothing*, and should any of them ask for the price of the articles, they are severely tortured."

There follows the case of a Brahmin, in which he, with others of his own village and of the neighbouring villages, was called on by the tahsildars to furnish planks, charcoal, firewood, etc., gratis, that he might carry on the Coleroon bridge-work; on refusing, he is seized by twelve men and maltreated in various ways. He adds:

"I presented a complaint to the Sub-Collector, Mr. W. Cadell, but he made no inquiry, and tore my complaint. As he is desirous of completing cheaply in Coleroon Bridge-work at the expense of the poor and of acquiring a good name from the Government, whatever may be the nature of the murder committed by the tahsildar, he takes no cognizance of it."

The light in which illegal practices, carried to the last degree of extortion and violence, were looked upon by the highest authority, is best shown by the case of Mr. Brereton, the Commissioner in charge of the Ludhiana District in the Punjab in 1855. According to the Report of the Chief Commissioner for the Punjab,* it was proved that

"In matters under the immediate cognizance or direction of the Deputy Commissioner, Mr. Brereton himself, the houses of wealthy citizens had been causelessly searched; that property seized on such occasions was detained for lengthened periods; that many parties were thrown into prison, and lay there for weeks, without charges being exhibited against them; and that the laws relating to security for bad character had been applied with sweeping and indiscriminating severity. That the Deputy Commissioner had been followed about from district to district by certain police officers and informers, whom he employed wherever he went, and that these men had been the main authors of mischief."

In his minute on the case, Lord Dalhousie says:

"We have irrefragable proof—proof, indeed, undisputed by Mr. Brereton himself—that that officer has been guilty of each item in the heavy catalogue of irregularities and illegalities with which the Chief Commissioner has charged him, and which have brought disgrace on one portion of the British administration, and have subjected a large number of British subjects to gross injustice, to arbitrary imprisonment and cruel torture."

Lord Dalhousie proposes "to make a great public example", and, consequently, is of opinion that

---

* John Lawrence.—*Ed.*

"Mr. Brereton cannot, *for the present*, be fitly intrusted with the authority of a Deputy Commissioner, but ought to be removed from that grade to the grade of a first class Assistant."

These extracts from the Blue Books may be concluded with the petition from the inhabitants of talook in Canara, on the Malabar coast, who, after stating that they had presented several petitions to the Government to no purpose, thus contrast their former and present condition:

"While we were cultivating wet and dry lands, hill tracts, low tracts and forests, paying the light assessment fixed upon us, and thereby enjoying tranquility and happiness under the administration of 'Ranee', Bahadur and Tippoo, the then Circar servants, levied an additional assessment, but we never paid it. We were not subjected to privations, oppressions or ill-usages in collecting the revenue. On the surrender of this country to the Honourable Company,* they devised all sorts of plans to squeeze out money from us. With this pernicious object in view, they invented rules and framed regulations, and directed their collectors and civil judges to put them in execution. But the then collectors and their subordinate native officials paid for some time due attention to our grievances, and acted in consonance with our wishes. On the contrary, the present collectors and their subordinate officials, *desirous of obtaining promotion on any account whatever*, neglect the welfare and interests of the people in general, turn a deaf ear to our grievances, and subject us to all sorts of oppressions."

We have here given but a brief and mildly-coloured chapter from the real history of British rule in India. In view of such facts, dispassionate and thoughtful men may perhaps be led to ask whether a people are not justified in attempting to expel the foreign conquerors who have so abused their subjects. And if the English could do these things in cold blood, is it surprising that the insurgent Hindus should be guilty, in the fury of revolt and conflict, of the crimes and cruelties alleged against them?

Written by K. Marx on August 28, 1857.
Published in the *New-York Daily Tribune*, No. 5120 of September 17, 1857, as a leading article.

Printed according to the newspaper text

* East India Company. —*Ed.*

K. Marx

*THE REVOLT IN INDIA

The mail of the *Baltic* reports no new events in India, but has a mass of highly interesting details, which we proceed to condense for the instruction of our readers. The first point to be noticed is that so late as the 15th of July the English had not got into Delhi. At the same time, the cholera had made its appearance in their camp, the heavy rains were setting in, and the raising of the siege and the withdrawal of the besiegers appeared to be a question of time only. The British press would fain make us believe that the pest, while carrying off Gen. Sir H. Barnard, had spared his worse-fed and harder-worked men. It is, therefore, not from explicit statements, communicated to the public, but only by way of inference from avowed facts, that we can arrive at some idea of the ravages of this terrible disease in the ranks of the besieging army. An officer in the camp before Delhi, writes, July 14:

> "We are doing nothing toward taking Delhi, and are merely defending ourselves against sorties of the enemy. We have parts of five European regiments, but can muster only 2,000 Europeans for any effective attack; large detachments from each regiment having been left to protect Jullundur, Ludhiana, Subathoo, Dugshale, Kussowlie, Ambala, Meerut and Phillaur. In fact, small detachments only of each regiment have joined us. The enemy are far superior to us in artillery."

Now this proves that the forces arriving from the Punjab found the great northern line of communication from Jullundur down to Meerut in a state of rebellion, and were consequently obliged to diminish their numbers by leaving detachments at the main posts. This accounts for the arrivals from the Punjab not mustering their anticipated strength, but it does not explain the reduction of the European force to 2,000 men. The Bombay correspondent of the London *Times*, writing on July 30, attempts to explain in another way the passive attitude of the besiegers. He says:

> "The reinforcements, indeed, have reached our camp — one wing of the 8th (King's), one of the 61st, a company of foot artillery, and two guns of a native troop, the 14th Irregular Cavalry Regiment (escorting a large ammunition train), the 2nd Punjab Cavalry, the 1st Punjab Infantry and the 4th Sikh Infantry; but the native portion of the troops thus added to the besieging force are not entirely and uniformly trustworthy, brigaded though they are with Europeans. The cavalry regiments of the Punjab force contain many Mussulmans and high caste Hindus, from Hindustan proper, and Rohilkhand, while the Bengal Irregular Cavalry are mainly composed of such elements. These men are, as a class, utterly disloyal, and their presence with the force in any numbers must be embarrassing — and so it has proved. In the 2nd Punjab Cavalry, it has been found necessary to disarm some 70 Hindustan men and to hang three, one a superior native officer. Of the 9th Irregulars, which have been some time with the force, several troopers have deserted, and the 4th Irregulars have, I believe, murdered their adjutant, while on detachment duty."

Here another secret is revealed. The camp before Delhi, it seems, bears some likeness to the camp of Agramante,[50] and the English have to struggle not only with the enemy in their front, but also with the ally in their lines. Still, this fact affords no sufficient cause for there being only 2,000 Europeans to be spared for offensive operations. A third writer, the Bombay correspondent of *The Daily News*,[51] gives an explicit enumeration of the forces assembled under Gen. Reed, Barnard's successor, which seems trustworthy, as he reckons up singly the different elements of which they are composed. According to his statement, about 1,200 Europeans and 1,600 Sikhs, irregular horse, etc., say altogether about 3,000 men, headed by Brigadier Gen. Chamberlain, reached the camp before Delhi from the Punjab between June 23 and July 3. On the other hand, he estimates the whole of the forces now assembled under Gen. Reed at 7,000 men, artillery and siege-train included, so that the army of Delhi, before the arrival of the Punjab reinforcements, could not have exceeded 4,000 men. The London *Times* of August 13, stated that Sir H. Barnard had collected an army of 7,000 British and 5,000 natives. Although this was a flagrant exaggeration, there is every reason to believe that the European forces then amounted to about 4,000 men, backed by a somewhat smaller number of natives. The original force, then, under Gen. Barnard, was as strong as the force now collected under Gen. Reed. Consequently, the Punjab reinforcements have only made up for the wear and tear which have reduced the strength of the besiegers almost one-half, an enormous loss, proceeding partly from the incessant sorties of the rebels, partly from the ravages of the cholera. Thus we understand why the British can muster only 2,000 Europeans for "any effective attack".

So much for the strength of the British forces before Delhi. Now for their operations. That they were not of a very brilliant character may be fairly inferred from the simple fact that, since June 8, when Gen. Barnard made his report on the capture of the height opposite Delhi, no bulletin whatever has been issued from headquarters. The operations, with a single exception, consist of sallies made by the besieged and repulsed by the besiegers. The besiegers were attacked now in front and then in the flanks, but mostly in the right rear. The sorties took place on the 27th and 30th of June, on the 3d, 4th, 9th and 14th of July. On the 27th of June, fighting was confined to outpost skirmishes, lasting some hours, but toward the afternoon was interrupted by a heavy fall of rain, the first of the season. On the 30th of June, the insurgents showed themselves in force among the inclosures on the right of the besiegers, harassing their pickets and supports. On the 3d of July, the besieged made early in the morning a feint attack on the right rear of the English position, then advanced several miles to that rear along the Karnal road as far as Alipore, in order to intercept a train of supplies and treasure under convoy to the camp. On their way, they encountered an outpost of the 2d Punjab Irregular Horse, which gave way at once. On their return to the city, on the 4th, the rebels were attacked by a body of 1,000 infantry and two squadrons of cavalry dispatched from the English camp to intercept them. They contrived, however, to effect their retreat with little or no loss and saving all their guns. On the 8th of July, a party was sent from the British camp to destroy a canal bridge at the village of Bussy, some six miles from Delhi, which in the former sallies had afforded the insurgents facilities for attacking the extreme British rear, and interfering with the British communications with Karnal and Meerut. The bridge was destroyed. On the 9th of July, the insurgents came out again in force and attacked the right rear of the British position. In the official accounts telegraphed to Lahore on the same day, the loss of the assailants is estimated at about one thousand killed; but this account seems much exaggerated, since we read in a letter of July 13 from the camp:

> "Our men buried and burnt two hundred and fifty of the enemy's dead, and large numbers were removed by themselves into the city."

The same letter, published in *The Daily News*, does not pretend that the British forced back the sepoys, but, on the contrary, that "the sepoys forced back all our working parties and then retired". The loss of the besiegers was considerable, amounting, as it did, to two hundred and twelve, killed and wounded. On the 14th of July, in consequence of another sortie, another fierce fight took place, the details of which have not yet arrived.

The besieged had, meanwhile, received strong reinforcements. On the 1st of July, the Rohilkhand mutineers from Bareilly, Moradabad and Shahjahanpur, consisting of four regiments of infantry, one of irregular cavalry, and one battery of artillery, had contrived to effect their junction with their comrades at Delhi.

> "It had been hoped," says the Bombay correspondent of the London *Times*, "that they would find the Ganges impassable but the anticipated rise of the river not taking place, it was crossed at Gurmukheser, the Doab was traversed and Delhi was attained. For two days, our troops had the mortification of watching the long train of men, guns, horses and beasts of burden of all kinds (for there was a treasure with the rebels, say £50,000) streaming across the bridge of boats into the city, without a possibility of preventing or in any way annoying them."

This successful march of the insurgents through the whole breadth of Rohilkhand proves all the country east of the Jumna up to the hills of Rohilkhand to be closed against the English forces, while the untroubled march of the insurgents from Neemuch to Agra, if connected with the revolts at Indore and Mhow, proves the same fact for all the country south-west of the Jumna and up to the Vindhya Mountains. The only successful — in fact, the only — operation of the English in regard to Delhi is the pacification of the country to its north and its north-west by Gen. Van Cortlandt's Punjab Sikh forces. Throughout the district between Ludhiana and Sirsa, he had mainly to encounter the robber tribes inhabiting villages sparsely scattered over a wild and sandy desert. On the 11th of July, he is said to have left Sirsa for Futtehabad, thence to march on Hissar, thus opening up the country in the rear of the besieging force.

Besides Delhi, three other points in the north-western provinces — Agra, Cawnpore and Lucknow — had become centres of the struggle between the natives and the English. The affair of Agra bears this peculiar aspect, that it shows for the first time the mutineers setting out on a deliberate expedition over about 300 miles of ground with the intention of attacking a distant English military station. According to *The Mofussilite*,[52] a journal printed at Agra, the sepoy regiments of Nasirabad and Neemuch, about 10,000 strong (say 7,000 infantry, 1,500 cavalry and 8 guns), approached Agra at the end of June, encamped in the beginning of July on a plain in the rear of the village of Sussia, about 20 miles from Agra, and on the 4th of July seemed preparing an attack on the city. On this news, the European residents in the cantonments before Agra took refuge in the fort. The commander at Agra* dispatched at first the Kotah contingent of horse, foot and artillery to serve as an advanced post against the enemy, but, having reached their place of destination, one and all bolted to join the ranks of the rebels. On July 5, the Agra garrison, consisting of the 3d Bengal Europeans, a battery of artillery and a corps of European volunteers, marched out to attack the mutineers, and are said to have driven them out of the village into the plain behind it, but were evidently themselves in their turn forced back, and, after a loss of 49 killed and 92 wounded, of a total force of 500 men engaged, had to retire, being harassed and threatened by the cavalry of the enemy with such activity as to prevent their "getting a shot at them", as *The Mofussilite* says. In other words, the English took to downright flight and shut themselves up in their fort, while the sepoys, advancing to Agra, destroyed nearly all the houses in the cantonment. On the following day, July 6, they proceeded to Bharatpur, on the way to Delhi. The important result of this affair is the interruption by the mutineers of the English line of communication between Agra and Delhi, and their probable appearance before the old city of the Moguls.

At Cawnpore, as was known from the last mail, a force of about 200 Europeans, under the command of Gen. Wheeler, having with them the wives and children of the 32d Foot, was shut up in a fortified work and surrounded by an overwhelming mass of rebels, headed by Nana Sahib of Bithur. Different assaults on the fort took place on the 17th and between the 24th and 28th of June, in the last of which, Gen. Wheeler was shot through the leg and died of his wounds. On June 28 Nana Sahib invited the English to surrender on the condition of being allowed to depart on boats down the Ganges to Allahabad. These terms were accepted, but the British had hardly put out into the middle of the stream when guns opened upon them

* John Colin. —*Ed.*

from the right bank of the Ganges. The people in the boats that tried to escape to the opposite bank were caught and cut down by a body of cavalry. The women and children were made captives. Messengers having been dispatched several times from Cawnpore to Allahabad with pressing demands for relief, on July 1 a column of Madras fusiliers and Sikhs started, under Major Renaud, on the way to Cawnpore. Within four miles of Fatehpur it was joined, on July 13 at daybreak, by Brig.-Gen. Havelock, who, at the head of about 1,300 Europeans of the 84th and 64th, the 13th Irregular Horse, and the remnant of Oudh Irregulars, reached Allahabad from Benares, July 3, and then followed up Major Renaud by forced marches. On the very day of his junction with Renaud, he was forced to accept battle before Fatehpur, whither Nana Sahib had led his native forces. After an obstinate engagement, Gen. Havelock, by a move in the flank of the enemy, succeeded in driving him out of Fatehpur in the direction of Cawnpore, where twice he had to encounter him again on the 15th and 16th of July. At the latter date, Cawnpore was recaptured by the English, Nana Sahib retreating to Bithur, situated on the Ganges, twelve miles distant from Cawnpore, and said to be strongly fortified. Before undertaking his expedition to Fatehpur, Nana Sahib had murdered all the captive English women and children. The recapture of Cawnpore was of the highest importance to the English, as it secured their Ganges line of communication.

At Lucknow, the capital of Oudh, the British garrison found themselves nearly in the same plight which had proved fatal to their comrades at Cawnpore —shut up in a fort, surrounded by overwhelming forces, straitened for provisions, and deprived of their leader. The latter, Sir H. Lawrence, died July 4, of tetanus, from a wound in the leg, received on the 2d, during a sortie. On the 18th and 19th of July, Lucknow was still holding out. Its only hope of relief rested on Gen. Havelock's pushing forward his forces from Cawnpore. The question is whether he would dare to do so with Nana Sahib in his rear. Any delay, however, must prove fatal to Lucknow, since the periodical rains would soon render field operations impossible.

The examination of these events forces the conclusion upon us that, in the north-western provinces of Bengal, the British forces were gradually drifting into the position of small posts planted on insulated rocks amid a sea of revolution. In Lower Bengal, there had occurred only partial acts of insubordination at Mirzapur, Dinapur and Patna, besides an unsuccessful attempt made by the roving Brahmins of the neighbourhood to recapture the holy city of Benares. In the Punjab, the spirit of rebellion was forcibly kept down, a mutiny being suppressed at Sealkote, another at Jhelum, and the disaffection of Peshawar successfully checked. Emeutes had already been attempted in Gujarat, at Pandharpur in Satara, at Nagpur and Sagar in the Nagpur territory, at Hyderabad in the Nizam's territory, and, lastly, as far south as Mysore, so that the calm of the Bombay and Madras presidencies must be understood as by no means perfectly secure.

Written by K. Marx on September 1, 1857.
Published in the *New-York Daily Tribune*, No. 5118 of September 15, 1857, as a leading article.

Printed according to the newspaper text

K. Marx

*BRITISH INCOMES IN INDIA

The present state of affairs in Asia suggests the inquiry, What is the real value of their Indian dominion to the British nation and people? Directly, that is in the shape of tribute, or surplus of Indian receipts over Indian expenditures, nothing whatever reaches the British Treasury. On the contrary, the annual outgo is very large. From the moment that the East India Company entered extensively on the career of conquest — now just about a century ago — their finances fell into an embarrassed condition, and they were repeatedly compelled to apply to Parliament, not only for military aid to assist them in holding the conquered territories, but for financial aid to save them from bankruptcy. And so things have continued down to the present moment, at which so large a call is made for troops on the British nation, to be followed, no doubt, by corresponding calls for money. In prosecuting its conquests hitherto, and building up its establishments, the East India Company has contracted a debt of upward of £50,000,000 sterling, while the British Government has been at the expense, for years past, of transporting to and from and keeping up in India, in addition to the forces, native and European, of the East India Company, a standing army of thirty thousand men. Such being the case, it is evident that the advantage to Great Britain from her Indian Empire must be limited to the profits and benefits which accrue to individual British subjects. These profits and benefits, it must be confessed, are very considerable.

First, we have the stockholders in the East India Company, to the number of about 3,000 persons, to whom under the recent Charter[53] there is guaranteed, upon a paid-up capital of six millions of pounds sterling, an annual dividend of ten and a half per cent, amounting to £630,000 annually. As the East India stock is held in transferable shares, anybody may become a stockholder who has money enough to buy the stock, which, under the existing Charter, commands a premium of from 125 to 150 per cent. Stock to the amount of £500, costing say $6,000, entitles the holder to speak at the proprietors' meetings, but to vote he must have £1,000 of stock. Holders of £ 3,000 have two votes, of £6,000 three votes, and of £10,000 or upward four votes. The proprietors, however, have but little voice, except in the election of the Board of Directors, of whom they choose twelve, while the Crown appoints six; but these appointees of the Crown must be qualified by having resided for ten years or more in India. One-third of the Directors go out of office each year, but may be re-elected or reappointed. To be a Director, one must be a proprietor of £2,000 of stock. The Directors have a salary of £500 each, and their Chairman and Deputy Chairman twice as much; but the chief inducement to accept the office is the great patronage attached to it in the appointment of all Indian officers, civil, and military—a patronage, however, largely shared, and, as to the most important offices, engrossed substantially, by the Board of Control. This Board consists of six members, all Privy Councilors, and in general two or three of them Cabinet Ministers—the President of the Board being always so, in fact a Secretary of State for India.

Next come the recipients of this patronage, divided into five classes—civil, clerical, medical, military and naval. For service in India, at least in the civil line, some knowledge of the languages spoken there is necessary, and to prepare young men to enter their civil service, the East India Company has a college at Haileybury. A corresponding college for the military service, in which, however, the rudiments of military science are the principal branches taught, has been established at Addiscombe, near London. Admission to these colleges was formerly a matter of favour on the part of the Directors of the Company, but under the latest modifications of the Charter it has been opened to competition in the way of a public examination of candidates. On first reaching India, a civilian is allowed about $150 a month, till having passed a necessary examination in one or more of the native languages (which must be within twelve months after his arrival), he is attached to the service with emoluments which vary from $2,500 to near $50,000 per annum. The latter is the pay of the members of the Bengal

Council; the members of the Bombay and Madras Councils receive about $30,000 per annum. No person not a member of Council can receive more than about $25,000 per annum, and, to obtain an appointment worth $20,000 or over, he must have been a resident in India for twelve years. Nine years' residence qualifies for salaries of from $15,000 to $ 20,000, and three years' residence for salaries of from $ 7,000 to $15,000. Appointments in the civil service go nominally by seniority and merit, but really to a great extent by favour. As they are the best paid, there is great competition to get them, the military officers leaving their regiments for this purpose whenever they can get a chance. The average of all the salaries in the civil service is stated at about $8,000, but this does not include perquisites and extra allowances, which are often very considerable. These civil servants are employed as Governors, Councilors, Judges, Ambassadors, Secretaries, Collectors of the Revenue, etc.—the number in the whole being generally about 800. The salary of the Governor-General of India is $125,000, but the extra allowances often amount to a still larger sum. The Church service includes three bishops and about one hundred and sixty chaplains. The Bishop of Calcutta has $25,000 a year; those of Madras and Bombay half as much; the chaplains from $2,500 to $7,000, besides fees. The medical service includes some 800 physicians and surgeons, with salaries of from $1,500 to $ 10,000.

The European military officers employed in India, including those of the contingents which the dependent princes are obliged to furnish, number about 8,000. The fixed pay in the infantry is, for ensigns, $1,080; lieutenants, $1,344; captains, $ 2,226; majors, $3,810; lieutenant-colonels, $5,520; colonels, $7,680. This is the pay in cantonment. In active service, it is more. The pay in the cavalry, artillery and engineers, is somewhat higher. By obtaining staff situations or employments in the civil service, many officers double their pay.

Here are about ten thousand British subjects holding lucrative situations in India, and drawing their pay from the Indian service. To these must be added a considerable number living in England, whither they have retired upon pensions, which in all the services are payable after serving a certain number of years. These pensions, with the dividends and interest on debts due in England, consume some fifteen to twenty millions of dollars drawn annually from India, and which may in fact be regarded as so much tribute paid to the English

Government indirectly through its subjects. Those who annually retire from the several services carry with them very considerable amounts of savings from their salaries, which is so much more added to the annual drain on India.

Besides those Europeans actually employed in the service of the Government, there are other European residents in India to the number of 6,000 or more, employed in trade or private speculation. Except a few indigo, sugar and coffee planters in the rural districts, they are principally merchants, agents and manufacturers, who reside in the cities of Calcutta, Bombay and Madras, or their immediate vicinity. The foreign trade of India, including imports and exports to the amount of about fifty millions of dollars of each, is almost entirely in their hands, and their profits are no doubt very considerable.

It is thus evident that individuals gain largely by the English connection with India, and of course their gain goes to increase the sum of the national wealth. But against all this a very large offset is to be made. The military and naval expenses paid out of the pockets of the people of England on Indian account have been constantly increasing with the extent of the Indian dominion. To this must be added the expense of Burmese, Afghan, Chinese and Persian wars. In fact, the whole cost of the late Russian war may fairly be charged to the Indian account, since the fear and dread of Russia, which led to that war, grew entirely out of jealousy as to her designs on India. Add to this the career of endless conquest and perpetual aggression in which the English are involved by the possession of India, and it may well be doubted whether, on the whole, this dominion does not threaten to cost quite as much as it can ever be expected to come to.

Written by K. Marx at the beginning of September, 1857.
Published in the *New-York Daily Tribune*, No. 5123 of September 21, 1857, as a leading article.

Printed according to the newspaper text

K. Marx

THE INDIAN REVOLT

London, September 4, 1857

The outrages committed by the revolted sepoys in India are indeed appalling, hideous, ineffable—such as one is prepared to meet only in wars of insurrection, of nationalities, of races, and above all of religion; in one word, such as respectable England used to applaud when perpetrated by the Vendeans on the "Blues", by the Spanish guerrillas on the infidel Frenchmen, by Serbians on their German and Hungarian neighbours, by Croats on Viennese rebels, by Cavaignac's Garde Mobile or Bonaparte's Decembrists on the sons and daughters of proletarian France.[54] However infamous the conduct of the sepoys, it is only the reflex, in a concentrated form, of England's own conduct in India, not only during the epoch of the foundation of her Eastern Empire, but even during the last ten years of a long-settled rule. To characterize that rule, it suffices to say that torture formed an organic institution of its financial policy.* There is something in human history like retribution; and it is a rule of historical retribution that its instrument be forged not by the offended, but by the offender himself.

The first blow dealt to the French monarchy proceeded from the nobility, not from the peasants. The Indian revolt does not commence with the ryots, tortured, dishonoured and stripped naked by the British, but with the sepoys, clad, fed, petted, fatted and pampered by them. To find parallels to the sepoy atrocities, we need not, as some London papers pretend, fall back on the middle ages, nor even wander beyond the history of contemporary England. All we want is to study the first Chinese

* See this collection, pp. 63-67. —*Ed.*

war,[55] an event, so to say, of yesterday. The English soldiery then committed abominations for the mere fun of it; their passions being neither sanctified by religious fanaticism nor exacerbated by hatred against an overbearing and conquering race, nor provoked by the stern resistance of a heroic enemy. The violations of women, the spittings of children, the roastings of whole villages, were then mere wanton sports, not recorded by mandarins, but by British officers themselves.

Even at the present catastrophe it would be an unmitigated mistake to suppose that all the cruelty is on the side of the sepoys, and all the milk of human kindness flows on the side of the English. The letters of the British officers are redolent of malignity. An officer writing from Peshawar gives a description of the disarming of the 10th Irregular Cavalry for not charging the 55th Native Infantry when ordered to do so. He exults in the fact that they were not only disarmed, but stripped of their coats and boots, and after having received 12d. per man, were marched down to the riverside, and there embarked in boats and sent down the Indus, where the writer is delighted to expect every mother's son will have a chance of being drowned in the rapids. Another writer informs us that some inhabitants of Peshawar having caused a night alarm by exploding little mines of gunpowder in honour of a wedding (a national custom), the persons concerned were tied up next morning, and "received such a flogging as they will not easily forget". News arrived from Pindee that three native chiefs were plotting. Sir John Lawrence replied by a message ordering a spy to attend to the meeting. On the spy's report, Sir John sent a second message, "Hang them". The chiefs were hanged. An officer in the civil service, from Allahabad, writes: "We have power of life and death in our hands, and we assure you we spare not." Another, from the same place: "Not a day passes but we string up from ten to fifteen of them (non-combatants)." One exulting officer writes: "Holmes is hanging them by the score, like a 'brick'." Another, in allusion to the summary hanging of a large body of the natives: "Then our fun commenced." A third: "We hold court-martials on horseback, and every nigger we meet with we either string up or shoot." From Benares we are informed that thirty zemindars were hanged on the mere suspicion of sympathizing with their own countrymen, and whole villages were burned down on the same plea. An officer from Benares, whose letter is printed in the London *Times*, says: "The European troops have become fiends when opposed to natives."

And then it should not be forgotten that, while the cruelties of the English are related as acts of martial vigour, told simply, rapidly, without dwelling on disgusting details, the outrages of the natives, shocking as they are, are still deliberately exaggerated. For instance, the circumstantial account first appearing in *The Times*, and then going the round of the London press, of the atrocities perpetrated at Delhi and Meerut, from whom did it proceed? From a cowardly parson residing at Bangalore, Mysore, more than a thousand miles, as the bird flies, distant from the scene of action. Actual accounts of Delhi evince the imagination of an English parson to be capable of breeding greater horrors than even the wild fancy of a Hindu mutineer. The cutting of noses, breasts, etc., in one word, the horrid mutilations committed by the sepoys, are of course more revolting to European feeling than the throwing of red-hot shell on Canton dwellings by a Secretary of the Manchester Peace Society,* or the roasting of Arabs pent up in a cave by a French Marshal,[56] or the flaying alive of British soldiers by the cat-o'-nine-tails under drum-head courtmartial, or any other of the philanthropical appliances used in British penitentiary colonies. Cruelty, like every other thing, has its fashion, changing according to time and place. Caesar, the accomplished scholar, candidly narrates how he ordered many thousand Gallic warriors[57] to have their right hands cut off. Napoleon would have been ashamed to do this. He preferred dispatching his own French regiments, suspected of republicanism, to Santo Domingo, there to die of the blacks and the plague.

The infamous mutilations committed by the sepoys remind one of the practices of the Christian Byzantine Empire, or the prescriptions of Emperor Charles V's[58] criminal law, or the English punishments for high treason, as still recorded by Judge Blackstone.[59] With Hindus, whom their religion has made virtuosi in the art of self-torturing, these tortures inflicted on the enemies of their race and creed appear quite natural, and must appear still more so to the English, who, only some years since, still used to draw revenues from the Juggernaut festivals, protecting and assisting the bloody rites of a religion of cruelty.

The frantic roars of the "bloody old *Times*", as Cobbett used to call it—its playing the part of a furious character in one of Mozart's operas, who indulges in most melodious strains in the

---

* Bowring. —*Ed.*

idea of first hanging his enemy, then roasting him, then quartering him, then spitting him, and then flaying him alive[60] — its tearing the passion of revenge to tatters and to rags — all this would appear but silly if under the pathos of tragedy there were not distinctly perceptible the tricks of comedy. The London *Times* overdoes its part, not only from panic. It supplies comedy with a subject even missed by Molière, the Tartuffe of Revenge. What it simply wants is to write up the funds and to screen the Government. As Delhi has not, like the walls of Jericho,[61] fallen before mere puffs of wind, John Bull is to be steeped in cries for revenge up to his very ears, to make him forget that his Government is responsible for the mischief hatched and the colossal dimensions it had been allowed to assume.

Written by K. Marx on September 4, 1857.
Published in the *New-York Daily Tribune*, No. 5119 of September 16, 1857.

Printed according to the newspaper text

K. Marx

*THE REVOLT IN INDIA

The news from India, which reached us yesterday, wears a very disastrous and threatening aspect for the English, though, as may be seen in another column, our intelligent London correspondent regards it differently.[62] From Delhi we have details to July 29, and a later report, to the effect that, in consequence of the ravages of the cholera, the besieging forces were compelled to retire from before Delhi and take up their quarters at Agra. It is true, this report is admitted by none of the London journals, but we can, at the very utmost, only regard it as somewhat premature. As we know from all the Indian correspondence, the besieging army had suffered severely in sorties made on the 14th, 18th and 23d of July. On those occasions the rebels fought with more reckless vehemence than ever, and with a great advantage from the superiority of their cannon.

"We are firing," writes a British officer, "18 pounders and 8-inch howitzers, and the rebels are replying with twenty-fours and thirty twos." "In the eighteen sallies," says another letter, "which we have had to stand, we have lost one-third of our numbers in killed and wounded."

Of reinforcements all that could be excepted was a body of Sikhs under Gen. Van Cortlandt. Gen. Havelock, after fighting several successful battles, was forced to fall back on Cawnpore, abandoning, for the time, the relief of Lucknow. At the same time "the rains had set in heavily before Delhi", necessarily adding to the virulence of the cholera. The dispatch which announces the retreat to Agra and the abandonment, for the moment, at least, of the attempt to reduce the capital of the Great Mogul, must, then, soon prove true, if it is not so already.

On the line of the Ganges the main interest rests on the

operations of Gen. Havelock, whose exploits at Fatehpur, Cawnpore and Bithur have naturally been rather extravagantly praised by our London contemporaries. As we have stated above, after having advanced twenty-five miles from Cawnpore, he found himself obliged to fall back upon that place in order not only to deposit his sick, but to wait for reinforcements. This is a cause for deep regret, for it indicates that the attempt at a rescue of Lucknow has been baffled. The only hope for the British garrison of the place is now in the force of 3,000 Gurkhas sent from Nepal to their relief by Jang Bahadur. Should they fail to raise the siege, then the Cawnpore butchery will be re-enacted at Lucknow. This will not be all. The capture by the rebels of the fortress of Lucknow, and the consequent consolidation of their power in Oudh, would threaten in the flank all British operations against Delhi, and decide the balance of the contending forces at Benares, and the whole district of Bihar. Cawnpore would be stripped of half its importance and menaced in its communications with Delhi on the one side, and with Benares on the other, by the rebels holding the fortress of Lucknow. This contingency adds to the painful interest with which news from that locality must be looked for. On the 16th of June the garrison estimated their powers of endurance at six weeks on famine allowance. Up to the last date of the dispatches, five of these weeks had already elapsed. Everything there now depends on the reported, but not yet certain reinforcements from Nepal.

If we pass lower down the Ganges, from Cawnpore to Benares and the district of Bihar, the British prospect is still darker. A letter in *The Bengal Gazette*,[63] dated Benares, August 3, states

> "that the mutineers from Dinapur, having crossed the Sohan, marched upon Arrah. The European inhabitants, justly alarmed for their safety, wrote to Dinapur for reinforcements. Two steamers were accordingly dispatched with detachments of her Majesty's 5th, 10th and 37th. In the middle of the night one of the steamers grounded in the mud and stuck fast. The men were hastily landed, and pushed forward on foot, but without taking due precautions. Suddenly they were assailed on both sides by a close and heavy fire, and 150 of their small force, including several officers, put *hors de combat*. It is supposed that all the Europeans at the station, about 47 in number, have been massacred."

Arrah, in the British district of Shahabad, Presidency of Bengal, is a town on the road from Dinapur to Ghasipur, twenty-five miles west of the former, seventy-five east of the latter. Benares itself was threatened. This place has a fort constructed upon European principles, and would become another Delhi if it fell into the hands of the rebels. At Mirzapur, situated to the south of Benares, and on the opposite bank of the Ganges, a Mussulman conspiracy has been detected; while at Berhampore, on the Ganges, some eighty miles distant from Calcutta, the 63d Native Infantry had been disarmed. In one word, disaffection on the one side and panic on the other were spreading throughout the whole Presidency of Bengal, even to the gates of Calcutta, where painful apprehensions prevailed of the great fast of the Muharram, when the followers of Islam, wrought up into a fanatical frenzy, go about with swords ready to fight on the smallest provocation, being likely to result in a general attack upon the English, and where the Governor-General* has felt himself compelled to disarm his own bodyguard. The reader will, then, understand at once that the principal British line of communications, the Ganges line, is in danger of being interrupted, intersected and cut off. This would bear on the progress of the reinforcements to arrive in November, and would isolate the British line of operations on the Jumna.

In the Bombay Presidency, also, affairs are assuming a very serious aspect. The mutiny at Kolhapur of the 27th Bombay Native Infantry is a fact, but their defeat by the British troops is a rumour only. The Bombay native army has broken out into successive mutinies at Nagpur, Aurangabad, Hyderabad, and, finally, at Kolhapur. The actual strength of the Bombay native army is 43,048 men, while there are, in fact, only two European regiments in that presidency. The native army was relied upon not only to preserve order within the limits of the Bombay Presidency, but to send reinforcements up to Scinde in the Punjab, and to form the columns moved on Mhow and Indore, to recover and hold those places, to establish communications with Agra, and relieve the garrison at that place. The column of Brigadier Stewart, charged with this operation, was composed of 300 men of the 3d Bombay European Regiment, 250 men of the 5th Bombay Native Infantry, 1,000 of the 25th Bombay Native Infantry, 200 of the 19th Bombay Native Infantry, 800 of the 3d Cavalry Regiment of the Hyderabad contingent. There are with this force, amounting to 2,250 native soldiers, about 700 Europeans, composed chiefly of the Queen's 86th Foot and the 14th Queen's Light Dragoons. The English had, moreover, assembled a column of the native army at Aurangabad to

* Charles John Canning. —*Ed.*

intimidate the disaffected territories of Khandesh and Nagpur, and at the same time form a support for the flying columns acting in Central India.

In that part of India we are told that "tranquillity is restored", but on this result we cannot altogether rely. In fact it is not the occupation of Mhow which decides that question, but the course pursued by the Holkar and Sindhia, the two Mahratta princes. The same dispatch which informs us of Stewart's arrival at Mhow adds that, although the Holkar still remained staunch, his troops had become unmanageable. As to the Sindhia's policy, not a word is dropped. He is young, popular, full of fire, and would be regarded as the natural head and rallying point for the whole Mahratta nation. He has 10,000 well-disciplined troops of his own. His defection from the British would not only cost them Central India, but give immense strength and consistency to the revolutionary league. The retreat of the forces before Delhi, the menaces and solicitations of the malcontents may at length induce him to side with his countrymen. The main influence, however, on the Holkar as well as the Sindhia, will be exercised by the Mahrattas of the Deccan, where, as we have already stated,* the rebellion has at last decidedly raised its head. It is here, too, that the festival of the Muharram is particularly dangerous. There is, then, some reason to anticipate a general revolt of the Bombay army. The Madras army, too, amounting to 60,555 native troops, and recruited from Hyderabad, Nagpur, Malwa, the most bigoted Mohammedan districts, would not be long in following the example. Thus, then, if it be considered that the rainy season during August and September will paralyze the movements of the British troops and interrupt their communications, the supposition seems rational that in spite of their apparent strength, the reinforcements sent from Europe, arriving too late, and in dribblets only, will prove inadequate to the task imposed upon them. We may almost expect, during the following campaign, a rehearsal of the Afghanistan disasters.[64]

Written by K. Marx on September 18, 1857. Published in the *New-York Daily Tribune*, No. 5134 of October 3, 1857, as a leading article.

Printed according to the newspaper text

---

* See this collection, p. 73.—*Ed.*

K. Marx

*THE REVOLT IN INDIA

The news received from India by the *Atlantic* yesterday has two prominent points, namely, the failure of Gen. Havelock to advance to the relief of Lucknow, and the persistence of the English at Delhi. This latter fact finds a parallel only in British annals, and in the Walcheren expedition.[65] The failure of that expedition having become certain toward the middle of August, 1809, they delayed re-embarking until November. Napoleon, when he learned that an English army had landed at that place, recommended that it should not be attacked, and that the French should leave its destruction to the disease sure to do them more injury than the cannon, without its costing one centime to France. The present Great Mogul, even more favoured than Napoleon, finds himself able to back the disease by his sallies and his sallies by the disease.

A British Government dispatch, dated Gagliari, Sept. 27, tells us that

> "the latest dates from Delhi are to the 12th of August, when that city was still in possession of the rebels; but that an attack was expected to be made shortly, as Gen. Nicholson was within a day's march with considerable reinforcements."

If Delhi is not taken till Wilson and Nicholson attack it with their present strength, its walls will stand till they fall of themselves. Nicholson's considerable forces amount to about 4,000 Sikhs—a reinforcement absurdly disproportionate for an attack upon Delhi, but just large enough to afford a new suicidal pretext for not breaking up the camp before the city.

After Gen. Hewitt had committed the fault, and one may even in a military point of view say the crime, of permitting the

Meerut rebels to make their way to Delhi, and after the two first weeks had been wasted, allowing an irregular surprise of that city, the planning of the siege of Delhi appears an almost incomprehensible blunder. An authority which we shall take the liberty of placing even above the military oracles of the London *Times*, Napoleon, lays down two rules of warfare looking almost like commonplaces: 1st. That "only what can be supported ought to be undertaken, and only what presents the greatest number of chances of success"; and 2dly. That "the main forces should be employed only where the main object of war, the destruction of the enemy, lies." In planning the siege of Delhi, these rudimental rules have been violated. The authorities in England must have been aware that the Indian Government itself had recently repaired the fortifications of Delhi so far that that city could be captured by a regular siege only, requiring a besieging force of at least 15,000 to 20,000 men, and much more, if the defence was conducted in an average style. Now, 15,000 to 20,000 men being requisite for this enterprise, it was downright folly to undertake it with 6,000 or 7,000. The English were further aware that a prolonged siege, a matter of course in consequence of their numerical weakness, would expose their forces in that locality, in that climate, and at that season, to the attacks of an invulnerable and invisible enemy, spreading the seeds of destruction among their ranks. The chances of success, therefore, were all against a siege of Delhi.

As to the object of the war, it was beyond doubt the maintenance of English rule in India. To attain that object, Delhi was a point of no strategical significance at all. Historical tradition, in truth, endowed it in the eyes of the natives with a superstitious importance, clashing with its real influence, and this was sufficient reason for the mutinous sepoys to single it out as their general place of rendezvous. But if, instead of forming their military plans according to the native prejudices, the English had left Delhi alone and isolated it, they would have divested it of its fancied influence; while, by pitching their tents before it, running their heads against it, and concentrating upon it their main force and the attention of the world, they cut themselves off from even chances of retreat, or rather gave to a retreat all the effects of a signal defeat. They have thus simply played into the hands of the mutineers who wanted to make Delhi the object of the campaign. But this is not all. No great ingenuity was required to convince the English that for them it was of prime importance to create an active field army, whose operations might stifle the sparks of disaffection, keep open the communications between their own military stations, throw the enemy upon some few points and isolate Delhi. Instead of acting upon this simple and self-evident plan, they immobilize the only active army at their disposal by concentrating it before Delhi, leave the open field to the mutineers, while their *own* garrisons hold scattered spots, disconnected, far distant from each other, and blocked up by overwhelming hostile forces allowed to take their own time.

By fixing their main mobile column before Delhi, the English have not choked up the rebels, but petrified their own garrisons. But, apart from this fundamental blunder at Delhi, there is hardly anything in the annals of war to equal the stupidity which directed the operations of these garrisons, acting independently, irrespectively of each other, lacking all supreme leadership, and acting not like members of one army, but like bodies belonging to different and even hostile nations. Take, for instance, the case of Cawnpore and Lucknow. There were two adjacent places, and two separate bodies of troops, both very small and disproportionate to the occasion, placed under separate commands, though they were only forty miles apart, and with as little unity of action between them as if situated at the opposite poles. The simplest rules of strategy would have required that Sir Hugh Wheeler, the military commander at Cawnpore, should be empowered to call Sir H. Lawrence, the Chief Commissioner of Oudh, with his troops, back to Cawnpore, thus to strengthen his own position while momentarily evacuating Lucknow. By this operation, *both* garrisons would have been saved, and by the subsequent junction of Havelock's troops with them, a little army been created able to check Oudh and to relieve Agra. Instead of this, by the independent action of the two places, the garrison of Cawnpore is butchered, the garrison of Lucknow is sure to fall with its fortress, and even the wonderful exertions of Havelock, marching his troops 126 miles in eight days, sustaining as many fights as his march numbered days, and performing all this in an Indian climate at the height of the summer season—even his heroic exertions are baffled. Having still more exhausted his overworked troops in vain attempts at the rescue of Lucknow, and being sure to be forced to fresh useless sacrifices by repeated expeditions from Cawnpore, executed on a constantly decreasing radius, he will, in all probability, have at last to retire upon Allahabad, with hardly any men at his back. The operations of his troops, better than anything else, show what even the small English army before Delhi would have been able to do if concentrated for action in the field, instead of being caught alive in the pestilential camp. Concentration is the secret of strategy. Decentralization is the plan adopted by the English in India. What they had to do was to reduce their garrisons to the smallest possible number, disencumber them at once of women and children, evacuate all stations not of strategical importance, and thus collected the greatest possible army in the field. Now, even the dribblets of reinforcements, sent up the Ganges from Calcutta, have been so completely absorbed by the numerous isolated garrisons that not one detachment has reached Allahabad.

As for Lucknow, the most gloomy previsions inspired by the recent previous mails* are now confirmed. Havelock has again been forced to fall back on Cawnpore; there is no possibility of relief from the allied Nepalese force; and we must now expect to hear of the capture of the place by starvation, and the massacre of its brave defenders with their wives and children.

Written by K. Marx on September 29, 1857.
Published in the *New-York Daily Tribune*, No. 5142 of October 13, 1857, as a leading article.

Printed according to the newspaper text

* See this collection, p. 84. —*Ed.*

K. Marx

*THE REVOLT IN INDIA[66]

In discussing the state of the Indian revolt they are full of the same optimism which they have cultivated from the beginning. We are not only told that a successful attack upon Delhi was to take place, but that it was to take place on the 20th of August. The first thing to ascertain is, of course, the present strength of the besieging force. An artillery officer, writing from the camp before Delhi on the 13th of August, gives the following detailed statement of the effective British forces on the 10th of that month:

	British Officers	British Troops	Native Officers	Native Troops	Horses
Staff	30	—	—	—	—
Artillery	39	598	—	—	—
Engineers	26	39	—	—	—
Cavalry	18	570	—	—	520
1st Brigade					
Her Majesty's 75th Regt.	16	502		—	—
Hon. Co.'s 2d Fusiliers	17	487	—	—	—
Kumaon Battalion	4	—	13	435	—
2d Brigade					
Her Majesty's 60th Rifles	15	251	—	—	—
Hon. Co.'s 2d Fusiliers	20	493	—	—	—
Timur Battalion	4	—	9	319	
3d Brigade					
Her Majesty's 8th Regt.	15	153	—	—	—
Her Majesty's 61st Regt.	12	249	—	—	—
4th Sikhs	4	—	4	365	—
Guide Corps	4	—	4	196	—
Coke's Corps	5	—	16	709	
Total	229	3,342	46	2,024	520

The total effective British force in the camp before Delhi amounted, therefore, on the 10th of August to exactly 5,641 men. From these we must deduct 120 men (112 soldiers and 8 officers), who, according to the English reports, fell on the 12th of August during the attack upon a new battery which the rebels had opened outside the walls, in front of the English left. There remained, then, the number of 5,521 fighting men when Brigadier Nicholson joined the besieging army with the following forces from Ferozepore, escorting a second-class siege-train: the 52d Light Infantry (say 900 men), a wing of the 61st (say 4 companies, 360 men), Bourchier's field battery, a wing of the 6th Punjab Regiment (say 540 men), and some Multan horse and foot; altogether a force of about 2,000 men, of whom somewhat more than 1,200 were Europeans. Now, if we add this force to the 5,521 fighting men who were in the camp on the junction of Nicholson's forces, we obtain a total of 7,521 men. Further reinforcements are said to have been dispatched by Sir John Lawrence, the Governor of the Punjab, consisting of the remaining wing of the 8th Foot, three companies of the 24th, with three horse-artillery guns of Captain Paton's troops from Peshawar, the 2d Punjab Infantry, the 4th Punjab Infantry, and the other wing of the 6th Punjab. This force, however, which we may estimate at 3,000 men, at the utmost, and the bulk of which consists altogether of Sikhs, had not yet arrived. If the reader can recall the arrival of the Punjab reinforcements under Chamberlain* about a month earlier, he will understand that, as the latter were only sufficient to bring Gen. Reed's army up to the original number of Sir H. Barnard's forces, so the new reinforcements are only sufficient to bring Brigadier Wilson's army up to the original strength of Gen. Reed; the only real fact in favour of the English being the arrival, at last, of a siege-train. But suppose even the expected 3,000 men to have joined the camp, and the total English force to have reached the number of 10,000, the loyalty of one-third of which is more than doubtful, what are they to do? They will invest Delhi, we are told. But leaving aside the ludicrous idea of investing with 10,000 men a strongly-fortified city, more than seven miles in extent, the English must first turn the Jumna from its regular course before they can think of investing Delhi. If the English entered Delhi in the morning, the rebels might leave it in the

* See this collection, p. 69. —*Ed.*

evening, either by crossing the Jumna and making for Rohilkhand and Oudh, or by marching down the Jumna in the direction of Muttra and Agra. At all events, the investment of a square, one of whose sides is inaccessible to the besieging forces, while affording a line of communication and retreat to the besieged, is a problem not yet solved.

"All agree," says the officer from whom we have borrowed the above table, "that taking Delhi by assault is out of the question."

He informs us, at the same time, what is really expected in the camp, viz.: "to shell the town for several days and make a decent breach." Now, this officer himself adds that,

"at a moderate calculation, the enemy must muster now nearly forty thousand men besides guns unlimited and well worked; their infantry also fighting well."

If the desperate obstinacy with which Mussulmans are accustomed to fight behind walls be considered, it becomes a great question indeed whether the small British army, having rushed in through "a decent breach", would be allowed to rush out again.

In fact, there remains only one chance for a successful attack upon Delhi by the present British forces—that of internal dissensions breaking out among the rebels, their ammunition being spent, their forces being demoralized, and their spirit of self-reliance giving way. But we must confess that their uninterrupted fighting from the 31st of July to the 12th of August seems hardly to warrant such a supposition. At the same time, a Calcutta letter gives us a broad hint why the English generals had resolved, in the teeth of all military rules, upon keeping their ground before Delhi.

"When," it says, "a few weeks ago it became a question whether our force should retreat from before Delhi, because it was too much harassed by daily fighting to support overwhelming fatigues much longer, that intention was strenuously resisted by Sir John Lawrence, who plainly informed the generals that their retreat would be the signal for the rising of the populations around them, by which they must be placed in imminent danger. This counsel prevailed, and Sir John Lawrence promised to send them all the reinforcements he could muster."

Denuded as it has been by Sir John Lawrence, the Punjab itself may now rise in rebellion, while the troops in the cantonments before Delhi are likely to be laid on their backs and decimated by the pestilential effluvia rising from the soil at the close of the rainy season. Of Gen. Van Cortlandt's forces, reported four weeks ago to have reached Hissar, and to be pushing forward to Delhi,* no more is heard. They must, then, have encountered serious obstacles, or have been disbanded on their route.

The position of the English on the Upper Ganges is, in fact, desperate. Gen. Havelock is threatened by the operations of the Oudh rebels, moving from Lucknow via Bithur and trying at Fatehpur, to the south of Cawnpore, to cut off his retreat; while simultaneously the Gwalior contingent is marching on Cawnpore from Kalpi, a town situated on the right bank of the Jumna. This concentric movement, perhaps directed by Nana Sahib, who is said to wield the supreme command at Lucknow, betrays for the first time some notion of strategy on the part of the rebels, while the English seem anxious only to exaggerate their own foolish method of centrifugal warfare. Thus we are told that the 90th Foot and the 5th Fusiliers dispatched from Calcutta to reinforce Gen. Havelock have been intercepted at Dinapur by Sir James Outram, who has taken it into his head to lead them via Fyzabad to Lucknow. This plan of operation is hailed by *The Morning Advertiser*[67] of London as the stroke of a master mind, because, it says, Lucknow will thus have been placed between two fires, being threatened on its right from Cawnpore and on its left from Fyzabad. According to the ordinary rules of war, the immensely weaker army, which, instead of trying to concentrate its scattered members, cuts itself up into two portions, separated by the whole breadth of the hostile army, has spared the enemy the pains of annihilating it. For Gen. Havelock, the question, in fact, is no longer to save Lucknow, but to save the remainder of his own and Gen. Neill's little corps. He will very likely have to fall back upon Allahabad. Allahabad is indeed a position of decisive importance, forming, as it does, the point of junction between the Ganges and the Jumna, and the key to the Doab, situated between the two rivers.

On the first glance at the map, it will be seen that the main line of operations for an English army attempting the reconquest of the north-western provinces runs along the valley of the Lower Ganges. The positions of Dinapur, Benares, Mirzapur, and, above all, of Allahabad, from which the real

* See this collection, p. 72. —*Ed.*

operations must commence, will therefore have to be strengthened by the withdrawal to them of the garrisons of all the smaller and strategically indifferent stations in the Province of Bengal proper. That this main line of operations itself is seriously threatened at this moment, may be seen from the following extract from a Bombay letter addressed to *The London Daily News*:

"The late mutiny of three regiments at Dinapur has cut off communications (except by steamers on the river) between Allahabad and Calcutta. The mutiny at Dinapur is the most serious affair that has happened lately, inasmuch as the whole of the Bihar district, within 200 miles of Calcutta, is now in a blaze. Today a report has arrived that the Santals have again risen, and the state of Bengal, overrun with 150,000 savages, who delight in blood, plunder and rapine, would be truly terrible."

The minor lines of operation, as long as Agra holds out, are those for the Bombay army, via Indore and Gwalior to Agra, and for the Madras army, via Sagar and Gwalior to Agra, with which latter place the Punjab army, as well as the corps holding Allahabad, require to have their lines of communication restored. If, however, the wavering princes of Central India should openly declare against the English, and the mutiny among the Bombay army assume a serious aspect, all military calculation is at an end for the present, and nothing will remain certain but an immense butchery from Cashmere to Cape Comorin. In the best case, all that can be done is to delay decisive events until the arrival in November of the European forces. Whether even this be effected will depend upon the brains of Sir Colin Campbell, of whom, till now, nothing is known but his personal bravery. If he is the man for his place, he will, at any expense, whether Delhi fall or not, create a disposable force, however small, with which to take the field. Yet, the ultimate decision, we must repeat, lies with the Bombay army.

Written by K. Marx on October 6, 1857. Published in the *New-York Daily Tribune*, No. 5151 of October 23, 1857, as a leading article.

Printed according to the newspaper text

K. Marx

*THE REVOLT IN INDIA

The mail of the *Arabia* brings us the important intelligence of the fall of Delhi. This event, so far as we can judge from the meagre details at hand, appears to have resulted upon the simultaneous occurrence of bitter dissensions among the rebels, a change in the numerical proportions of the contending parties, and the arrival on Sept. 5 of the siege-train which was expected as long ago as June 8.

After the arrival of Nicholson's reinforcements, we had estimated the army before Delhi at a total of 7,521 men,* an estimate fully confirmed since. After the subsequent accession of 3,000 Cashmere troops, lent to the English by the Rajah Ranbir Singh, the British forces are stated by *The Friend of India*[68] to have amounted in all to about 11,000 men. On the other hand, *The Military Spectator*[69] of London affirms that the rebel forces had diminished in numbers to about 17,000 men, of whom 5,000 were cavalry; while *The Friend of India* computes their forces at about 13,000, including 1,000 irregular cavalry. As the horse became quite useless after the breach was once effected and the struggle within the town had begun, and, consequently, on the very entrance of the English they made their escape, the total forces of the sepoys, whether we accept the computation of *The Military Spectator* or of *The Friend of India*, could not be estimated beyond 11,000 or 12,000 men. The English forces, less from increase on their side than from a decrease on the opposite one, had, therefore, become almost equal to those of the mutineers; their slight numerical inferiority

* See this collection, p. 92. —*Ed.*

being more than made up by the moral effect of a successful bombardment and the advantages of the offensive enabling them to choose the points on which to throw their main strength, while the defenders were obliged to disperse their inadequate forces over all the points of the menaced circumference.

The decrease on the part of the rebel forces was caused still more by the withdrawal of whole contingents in consequence of internal dissensions than by the heavy losses they suffered in their incessant sorties for a period of about ten days. While the Mogul spectre himself like the merchants of Delhi, had become averse to the rule of the sepoys, who plundered them of every rupee they had amassed, the religious dissensions between the Hindu and Mohammedan sepoys, and the quarrels between the old garrison and the new reinforcements, sufficed to break up their superficial organization and to insure their downfall. Still, as the English had to cope with a force but slightly superior to their own, without unity of command, enfeebled and dispirited by dissensions in their own ranks, but who yet, after 84 hours' bombardment, stood a six days' cannonade and street fight within the walls, and then quietly crossed the Jumna on the bridge of boats, it must be confessed that the rebels at last, with their main forces, made the best of a bad position.

The facts of the capture appear to be, that on Sept. 8 the English batteries were opened much in advance of the original position of their forces and within 700 yards of the walls. Between the 8th and the 11th British heavy ordnance guns and mortars were pushed forward still nearer to the works, a lodgement being effected and batteries established with little loss, considering that the Delhi garrison made two sorties on the 10th and 11th, and made repeated attempts to open fresh batteries, and kept up an annoying fire from rifle-pits. On the 12th the English sustained a loss of about 56 killed and wounded. On the morning of the 13th the enemy's expense magazine, on one bastion, was blown up, as also the wagon of a light gun, which enfiladed the British batteries from the Talvara suburbs; and the British batteries effected a practicable breach near the Cashmere gate. On the 14th the assault was made on the city. The troops entered at the breach near the Cashmere gate without serious opposition, gained possession of the large buildings in its neighbourhood and advanced along the ramparts to the Moree bastion and Kabul gate, when the resistance grew very obstinate, and the loss was consequently severe. Preparations were being made to turn the guns from the captured bastions on the city, and to bring up other guns and mortars to commanding points. On the 15th the Burn bastions and Lahore bastions were played upon by the captured guns on the Moree and Kabul bastions, while a breach was made in the magazine and the palace began to be shelled. The magazine was stormed at daylight, Sept. 16, while on the 17th the mortars continued to play upon the palace from the magazine inclosure.

At this date, owing, it is said by *The Bombay Courier,*[70] to the plunder of the Punjab and Lahore mails on the Scinde frontier, the official accounts of the storm break off. In a private communication addressed to the Governor of Bombay, it is stated that the entire city of Delhi was occupied on Sunday, the 20th, the main forces of the mutineers leaving the city at 3 a.m. on the same day, and escaping over the bridges of boats in the direction of Rohilkhand. Since a pursuit on the part of the English was impracticable until after the occupation of Selimgurh, situated on the river front, it is evident that the rebels, slowly fighting their way from the extreme north end of the city to its south-eastern extremity, kept, until the 20th, the position necessary for covering their retreat.

As to the probable effect of the capture of Delhi, a competent authority, *The Friend of India,* remarks that

> "it is the condition of Bengal, and not the state of Delhi, that ought at this time to engage the attention of Englishmen. The long delay that has taken place in the capture of the town has actually destroyed any prestige that we might have derived from an early success; and the strength of the rebels and their numbers are diminished as effectually by maintaining the siege as they would be by the capture of the city."

Meanwhile, the insurrection is said to be spreading northeast from Calcutta, through Central India up to the northwest; while on the Assam frontier, two strong regiments of Poorbeahs, openly proposing the restoration of the ex-Rajah Parandur Singh, had revolted; the Dinapur and Rangpur mutineers, led by Kower Singh, were marching by Banda and Nagod in the direction of Jubbulpore, and had forced, through his own troops, the Rajah of Rewa to join them. At Jubbulpore itself the 52nd Bengal Native Regiment had left their cantonments, taking with them a British officer as a hostage for their comrades left behind. The Gwalior mutineers are reported to have crossed the Chambal and are encamped somewhere between the river and Dholpur. The most serious items of intelligence remain to be noticed. The Jodhpur Legion has, it appears, taken service with the rebel Rajah of Arwah, a place 90 miles southwest of Beawar. They have defeated a considerable force which the Rajah of Jodhpur had sent against them, killing the General and Captain Monck Mason, and capturing three guns. Gen. G. St. P. Lawrence made an advance against them with some of the Nasirabad force, and compelled them to retreat into a town, against which, however, his further attempts proved unavailing. The denuding of Scinde of its European troops had resulted in a widely extended conspiracy, attempts at insurrection being made at no less than five different places, among which figure Hyderabad, Karachi and Shikarpur. There is also an untoward symptom in the Punjab, the communication between Multan and Lahore having been cut off for eight days.

In another place our readers will find a tabular statement of the forces dispatched from England since June 18; the days of arrival of the respective vessels being calculated by us on official statements, and therefore in favour of the British Government.[71] From that list it will be seen that, apart from the small detachments of artillery and engineers sent by the overland route, the whole of the army embarked amounts to 30,899 men, of whom 24,884 belong to the infantry, 3,826 to the cavalry, and 2,334 to the artillery. It will also be seen that before the end of October no considerable reinforcements were to be expected.

TROOPS FOR INDIA

The following is a list of the troops which have been sent to India from England since June 18, 1857

Date of Arrival	Total	Calcutta	Ceylon	Bombay	Karachi	Madras
September 20	214	214				
October 1	300	300				
October 15	1,906	124	1,782			
October 17	288	288				
October 20	4,235	3,845	390			
October 30	2,028	479	1,544			
Total for Oct.	8,757	5,036	3,721		—	—
November 1	3,495	1,234	1,629		632	
November 5	879	879				
November 10	2,700	904	340	400	1,056	
November 12	1,633	1,633				
November 15	2,610	2,132	478			
November 19	234	—	—	—	234	

Date of Arrival	Total	Calcutta	Ceylon	Bombay	Karachi	Madras
November 20	1,216	—	278	938	—	—
November 24	406	—	406	—	—	—
November 25	1,276	—	—	—	—	1,276
November 30	666	—	462	204	—	—
Total for Nov.	15,115	6,782	3,593	1,542	1,922	1,276
December 1	354	—	—	354	—	—
December 5	459	—	—	201	—	258
December 10	1,758	—	607	—	1,151	—
December 14	1,057	—	—	1,057	—	—
December 15	948	—	—	647	301	—
December 20	693	185	—	300	208	—
December 25	624	—	—	—	624	—
Total for Dec.	5,893	1,851	607	2,359	2,284	258
January 1	340	—	—	340	—	—
January 5	220	—	—	—	—	220
January 15	140	—	—	—	—	140
January 20	220	—	—	—	—	220
Total for Jan.	920	—	—	340	—	580
Sept. till Jan. 20	30,899	12,217	7,921	4,431	4,206	2,[illegible]
	Troops dispatched by overland route:					
October 2	235 R.E.	117	—	—	118	—
October 12	221 Art.	221	—	—	—	
October 14	224 R.E.	122	—	—	12[illegible]	—
Total for Oct.	700	460	—	—	240	

Total . . . .

Mon en route from Cape, partly arrived 4,000

Grand total 35,599

Written by K. Marx on October 30, 1857.
Published in the *New-York Daily Tribune*, No. 5170 of November 14, 1857, as a leading article.

Printed according to the newspaper text

F. Engels

*THE CAPTURE OF DELHI

We will not join in the noisy chorus which, in Great Britain, is now extolling to the skies the bravery of the troops that took Delhi by storm. No people, not even the French, can equal the English in self-laudation, especially when bravery is the point in question. The analysis of the facts, however, very soon reduces, in ninety-nine cases out of a hundred, the grandeur of this heroism to very commonplace proportions; and every man of common sense must be disgusted at this overtrading in other people's courage, by which the English paterfamilias who lives quietly at home, and is uncommonly averse to anything that threatens him with the remotest chance of obtaining military glory, attempts to pass himself off as a participator in the undoubted, but certainly not so very extraordinary, bravery shown in the assault on Delhi.

If we compare Delhi with Sevastopol, we of course agree that the sepoys were no Russians; that none of their sallies against the British cantonment was anything like Inkerman;[72] that there was no Totleben in Delhi, and that the sepoys, bravely as every individual man and company fought in most instances, were utterly without leadership, not only for brigades and divisions, but almost for battalions; that their cohesion did not therefore extend beyond the companies; that they entirely lacked the scientific element without which an army is nowadays helpless, and the defence of a town utterly hopeless. Still, the disproportion of numbers and means of action, the superiority of the sepoys over the Europeans in withstanding the climate, the extreme weakness to which the force before Delhi was at times reduced, make up for many of these differences, and render a fair parallel between the two sieges (to call these operations sieges) possible. Again we do not consider the storming of Delhi as an act of uncommon or extraheroic bravery, although as in every battle individual acts of high spirit no doubt occurred on either side, but we maintain that the Anglo-Indian army before Delhi has shown more perseverance, force of character, judgement and skill, than the English army when on its trial between Sevastopol and Balaklava.[73] The latter, after Inkerman, was ready and willing to re-embark, and no doubt would have done so if it had not been for the French. The former, when the season of the year, the deadly maladies consequent upon it, the interruption of the communications, the absence of all chance of speedy reinforcements, the condition of all Upper India, invited a withdrawal, did indeed consider the advisability of this step, but for all that, held out at its post.

When the insurrection was at its highest point, a movable column in Upper India was the first thing required. There were only two forces that could be thus employed — the small force of Havelock, which soon proved inadequate, and the force before Delhi. That it was, under these circumstances, a military mistake to stay before Delhi, consuming the available strength in useless fights with an unassailable enemy; that the army in motion would have been worth four times its value when at rest; that the clearing of Upper India, with the exception of Delhi, the re-establishing of the communication, the crushing of every attempt of the insurgents to concentrate a force, would have been obtained, and with it the fall of Delhi as a natural and easy consequence, are indisputable facts. But political reasons commanded that the camp before Delhi should not be raised. It is the wiseacres at headquarters who sent the army to Delhi that should be blamed — not the perseverance of the army in holding out when once there. At the same time we must not omit to state that the effect of the rainy season on this army was far milder than was to be anticipated, and that with anything like an average amount of the sickness consequent upon active operations at such a period, the withdrawal or the dissolution of the army would have been unavoidable. The dangerous position of the army lasted till the end of August. The reinforcements began to come in, while dissensions continued to weaken the rebel camp. In the beginning of September the siege-train arrived, and the defensive position was changed into an offensive one. On the 7th of September the first battery opened its fire, and on the evening of the 13th two practicable breaches were opened. Let us now examine what took place during this interval.

If we were to rely, for this purpose, on the official dispatch of Gen. Wilson, we should be very badly off indeed. This report is quite as confused as the documents issued from the English headquarters in the Crimea ever were. No man living could make out from that report the position of the two breaches, or the relative position and order in which the storming columns were arranged. As to the private reports, they are, of course, still more hopelessly confused. Fortunately one of those skilful scientific officers who deserve nearly the whole credit of the success, a member of the Bengal engineers and artillery, has given a report of what occurred, in *The Bombay Gazette*,[74] as clear and business-like as it is simple and unpretending. During the whole of the Crimean war not one English officer was found able to write a report as sensible as this. Unfortunately he got wounded on the first day of the assault, and then his letter stops. As to later transactions, we are, therefore, still quite in the dark.

The English had strengthened the defences of Delhi so far that they could resist a siege by an Asiatic army. According to our modern notions, Delhi was scarcely to be called a fortress, but merely a place secured against the forcible assault of a field force. Its masonry wall, 16 feet high and 12 feet thick, crowned by a parapet of 3 feet thickness and 8 feet height, offered 6 feet of masonry besides the parapet, uncovered by the glacis and exposed to the direct fire of the attack. The narrowness of this masonry rampart put it out of the question to place cannon anywhere, except in the bastions and Martello towers. These latter flanked the curtain but very imperfectly, and a masonry parapet of three feet thickness being easily battered down by siege guns (field pieces could do it), to silence the fire of the defence, and particularly the guns flanking the ditch, was very easy. Between wall and ditch there was a wide berm or level road, facilitating the formation of a practicable breach, and the ditch, under these circumstances, instead of being a *coupegorge* for any force that got entangled in it, became a resting place to re-form those columns that had got into disorder while advancing on the glacis.

To advance against such a place, with regular trenches, according to the rules of sieges, would have been insane, even if the first condition had not been wanting, viz., a force sufficient to invest the place on all sides. The state of the defences, the disorganization and sinking spirit of the defenders, would have rendered every other mode of attack than the one pursued an absolute fault. This mode is very well known to military men under the name of the forcible attack (*attaque de vive force*). The defences, being such only as to render an open attack impossible without heavy guns, are dealt with summarily by the artillery; the interior of the place is all the while shelled, and as soon as the breaches are practicable the troops advance to the assault.

The front under attack was the northern one, directly opposite to the English camp. This front is composed of two curtains and three bastions, forming a slightly reentering angle at the central (the Cashmere) bastion. The eastern position, from the Cashmere to the Water bastion, is the shorter one, and projects a little in front of the western position, between the Cashmere and the Moree bastions. The ground in front of the Cashmere and Water bastions was covered with low jungle, gardens, houses, etc., which had not been levelled down by the sepoys, and afforded shelter to the attack. (This circumstance explains how it was possible that the English could so often follow the sepoys under the very guns of the place, which was at that time considered extremely heroic, but was in fact a matter of little danger so long as they had this cover.) Besides, at about 400 or 500 yards from this front, a deep ravine ran in the same direction as the wall, so as to form a natural parallel for the attack. The river, besides, giving a capital basis to the English left, the slight salient formed by the Cashmere and Water bastions was selected very properly as the main point of attack. The western curtain and bastions were simultaneously subjected to a simulated attack, and this manoeuvre succeeded so well that the main force of the sepoys was directed against it. They assembled a strong body in the suburbs outside the Kabul gate, so as to menace the English right. This manoeuvre would have been perfectly correct and very effective, if the western curtain between the Moree and Cashmere bastions had been the most in danger. The flanking position of the sepoys would have been capital as a means of active defence, every column of assault being at once taken in flank by a movement of this force in advance. But the effect of this position could not reach as far eastward as the curtain between the Cashmere and Water bastions; and thus its occupation drew away the best part of the defending force from the decisive point.

The selection of the places for the batteries, their construction and arming, and the way in which they were served, deserve the greatest praise. The English had about 50 guns and mortars, concentrated in powerful batteries, behind good solid parapets. The sepoys had, according to official statements, 55 guns on the attacked front, but scattered over small bastions and Martello towers, incapable of concentrated action, and scarcely sheltered by the miserable three feet parapet. No doubt a couple of hours must have sufficed to silence the fire of the defence, and then there remained little to be done.

On the 8th, No. 1 battery, 10 guns, opened fire at 700 yards from the wall. During the following night the ravine aforesaid was worked out into a sort of trench. On the 9th, the broken ground and houses in front of this ravine were seized without resistance; and on the 10th, No. 2 battery, 8 guns, was unmasked. This latter was 500 or 600 yards from the wall. On the 11th, No. 3 battery, built very boldly and cleverly at 200 yards from the Water bastion in some broken ground, opened fire with six guns, while ten heavy mortars shelled the town. On the evening of the 13th the breaches — one in the curtain adjoining the right flank of the Cashmere bastion, and the other in the left face and flank of the Water bastion — were reported practicable for escalade, and the assault was ordered. The sepoys on the 11th had made a counter-approach on the glacis between the two menaced bastions, and threw out a trench for skirmishers about three hundred and fifty yards in front of the English batteries. They also advanced from this position outside the Kabul gate to flank attacks. But these attempts at active defence were carried out without unity, connection or spirit, and led to no result.

At daylight on the 14th five British columns advanced to the attack. One, on the right, to occupy the force outside the Kabul gate and attack, in case of success, the Lahore gate. One against each breach, one against the Cashmere gate, which was to be blown up, and one to act as a reserve. With the exception of the first, all these columns were successful.The breaches were but slightly defended, but the resistance in the houses near the wall was very obstinate. The heroism of an officer and three sergeants of the Engineers (for here there *was* heroism) succeeded in blowing open the Cashmere gate, and thus this entered also. By evening the whole northern front was in the possession of the English. Here Gen. Wilson, however, stopped. The indiscriminate assault was arrested, guns brought up and directed against every strong position in the town. With the exception of the storming of the magazine, there seems to have been very little actual fighting. The insurgents were dispirited and left the town in masses. Wilson advanced cautiously into town, found scarcely any resistance after the 17th, and occupied it completely on the 20th.

Our opinion on the conduct of the attack has been stated. As to the defence — the attempt at offensive counter-movements, the flanking position at the Kabul gate, the counter-approaches, the rifle-pits, all show that some notions of scientific warfare had penetrated among the sepoys; but either they were not clear enough, or not powerful enough, to be carried out with any effect. Whether they originated with Indians, or with some of the Europeans that are with them, is of course difficult to decide; but one thing is certain: that these attempts, though imperfect in execution, bear a close resemblance in their ground-work to the active defence of Sevastopol, and that their execution looks as if a correct plan had been made for the sepoys by some European officer, but that they had not been able to understand the idea fully, or that disorganization and want of command turned practical projects into weak and powerless attempts.

Written by F. Engels on November 16, 1857.
Published in the *New-York Daily Tribune*, No. 5188 of December 5, 1857, as a leading article.

Printed according to the newspaper text

K. Marx

THE APPROACHING INDIAN LOAN

London, January 22, 1858

The buoyancy in the London money market, resulting from the withdrawal of an enormous mass of capital from the ordinary productive investments, and its consequent transfer to the security markets, has, in the last fortnight, been somewhat lessened by the prospects of an impending *Indian loan* to the amount of eight or ten million pounds sterling. This loan, to be raised in England, and to be authorized by Parliament immediately on its assembling in February, is required to meet the claims upon the East India Company by its home creditors, as well as the extra expenditure for war materials, stores, transport of troops, etc., necessitated by the Indian revolt. In August, 1857, the British Government had, before the prorogation of Parliament, solemnly declared in the House of Commons that no such loan was intended, the financial resources of the Company being more than sufficient to meet the crisis. The agreeable delusion thus palmed on John Bull was, however, soon dispelled when it oozed out that by a proceeding of a very questionable character, the East India Company had laid hold on a sum of about £3,500,000 sterling, intrusted to them by different companies, for the construction of Indian railways; and had, moreover, secretly borrowed £1,000,000 sterling from the Bank of England, and another million from the London joint-stock banks. The public being thus prepared for the worst, the Government did no longer hesitate to drop the mask, and by semi-official articles in *The Times, Globe*,[75] and other governmental organs, avow the necessity of the loan.

It may be asked why a special act on the part of the legislative power is required for launching such a loan, and then, why such an event does create the least apprehension, since, on the contrary, every vent for British capital, seeking now in vain for profitable investment, should, under present circumstances, be considered a windfall, and a most salutary check upon the rapid depreciation of capital.

It is generally known that the commercial existence of the East India Company was terminated in 1834,[76] when its principal remaining source of commercial profits, the monopoly of the China trade, was cut off. Consequently, the holders of East India stock having derived their dividends, nominally, at least, from the trade profits of the Company, a new financial arrangement with regard to them had become necessary. The payment of the dividends, till then chargeable upon the commercial revenue of the Company, was transferred to its political revenue. The proprietors of East India stocks were to be paid out of the revenues enjoyed by the East India Company in its governmental capacity, and, by act of Parliament, the Indian stock, amounting to £6,000,000 sterling, bearing ten per cent interest, was converted into a capital not to be liquidated except at the rate of £200 for every £100 of stock. In other words, the original East India stock of £6,000,000 sterling was converted into a capital of £12,000,000 sterling, bearing five per cent interest, and chargeable upon the revenue derived from the taxes of the Indian people. The debt of the East India Company was thus, by a Parliamentary sleight of hand, changed into a debt of the Indian people. There exists, besides, a debt exceeding £50,000,000 sterling, contracted by the East India Company in India, and exclusively chargeable upon the state revenues of that country; such loans contracted by the Company in India itself having always been considered to lie beyond the district of parliamentary legislation, and regarded no more than the debts contracted by the colonial governments in Canada or Australia for instance.

On the other hand, the East India Company was prohibited from contracting interest-bearing debts in Great Britain herself, without the especial sanction of Parliament. Some years ago, when the Company set about establishing railways and electric telegraphs in India, it applied for the authorization of Indian bonds in the London market, a request which was granted to the amount of £7,000,000 sterling, to be issued in bonds bearing 4 per cent interest, and secured only on the Indian state revenues. At the commencement of the outbreak in India, this bond-debt stood at £3,894,400 sterling, and the very necessity of again applying to Parliament shows the East India Company to have, during the course of the Indian insurrection, exhausted its legal powers of borrowing at home.

Now it is no secret that before recurring to this step, the East India Company had opened a loan at Calcutta, which, however, turned out a complete failure. This proves, on the one hand, that Indian capitalists are far from considering the prospects of British supremacy in India in the same sanguine spirit which distinguishes the London press; and, on the other hand, exacerbates the feelings of John Bull to an uncommon pitch, since he is aware of the immense hoardings of capital having gone on for the last seven years in India, whither, according to a statement recently published by Messrs. Haggard £ Pixley, there has been shipped in 1856 and 1857, from the port of London alone, bullion to the amount of £21,000,000. The London *Times*, in a most persuasive strain, has taught its readers that

> "of all the incentives to the loyalty of the natives, that of making them our creditors was the least doubtful; while, on the other hand, among an impulsive, secretive and avaricious people no temptation to discontent or treachery could be stronger than that created by the idea that they were annually taxed to send dividends to wealthy claimants in other countries."

The Indians, however, appear not to understand the beauty of a plan which would not only restore English supremacy at the expense of Indian capital, but at the same time, in a circuitous way, open the native hoards to British commerce. If, indeed, the Indian capitalists were as fond of British rule as every true Englishman thinks it an article of faith to assert, no better opportunity could have been afforded them of exhibiting their loyalty and getting rid of their silver. The Indian capitalists shutting up their hoards, John Bull must open his mind to the dire necessity of defraying himself in the first instance, at least, the expenses of the Indian insurrection, without any support on the part of the natives. The impending loan constitutes, moreover, a precedent only, and looks like the first leaf in a book, bearing the title, *Anglo-Indian Home Debt.* It is no secret that what the East India Company wants are not eight millions, or ten millions, but twenty-five to thirty millions pounds, and even these as a first installment only, not for expenses to be incurred, but for debts already due. The deficient revenue for the last three years amounted to £5,000,000; the treasure plundered by the insurgents up the 15th October last, to £ 10,000,000, according to the statement of *The Phoenix*,[77] an Indian governmental paper; the loss of revenue in the north-eastern provinces, consequent upon the rebellion, to £ 5,000,000, and the war expenses to at least £10,000,000.

It is true that successive loans by the Indian Company, in the London money market, would raise the value of money and prevent the increasing depreciation of capital; that is to say, the further fall in the rate of interest; but such a fall is exactly required for the revival of British industry and commerce. Any artificial check put upon the downward movement of the rate of discount is equivalent to an enhancement in the cost of production and the terms of credit, which, in its present weak state, English trade feels itself unable to bear. Hence the general cry of distress at the announcement of the Indian loan. Though the parliamentary sanction adds no imperial guarantee to the loan of the Company, that guarantee, too, must be conceded, if money is not to be obtained on other terms; and despite all fine distinctions, as soon as the East India Company is supplanted by the British Government its debt will be merged into the British debt. A further increase of the large national debt seems, therefore, one of the first financial consequences of the Indian Revolt.

Written by K. Marx on January 23, 1858.
Published in the *New-York Daily Tribune*, No. 5243 of February 9, 1858.

Printed according to the newspaper text

F. Engels

WINDHAM'S DEFEAT[78]

While during the Crimean war all England was calling for a man capable of organizing and leading her armies, and while incapables like Raglan, Simpson and Codrington were intrusted with the office, there was a soldier in the Crimea endowed with the qualities required in a general. We mean Sir Colin Campbell, who is now daily showing in India that he understands his profession with a master's mind. In the Crimea, after having been allowed to lead his brigade at the Alma[79] where from the rigid linetactics of the British army he had no chance to show his capacities, he was cooped up in Balaklava and never once allowed to participate in the succeeding operations. And yet, his military talents had been clearly established in India long before, by no less an authority than the greatest general England has produced since Marlborough, by Sir Charles James Napier. But Napier was an independent man, too proud to stoop to the reigning oligarchy—and his recommendation was enough to make Campbell marked and distrusted.

Other men, however, gained distinctions and honours in that war. There was Sir William Fenwick Williams of Kars, who now finds it convenient to rest on the laurels acquired by impudence, self-puffing, and by defrauding Gen. Kmety of his well-earned fame. A baronetcy, a thousand a year, a comfortable berth at Woolwich, and a seat in Parliament, are quite sufficient to prevent him risking his reputation in India. Unlike him, "the hero of the Redan",[80] Gen. Windham, has set out to command a division against the sepoys, and his very first act has settled him for ever. This same Windham, an obscure colonel of good family connections, commanded a brigade at the assault of the

Redan, during which operation he behaved extremely phlegmatically, and at last, no reinforcement arriving, twice left his troops to shift for themselves, while he went to inquire about them himself. For this very questionable act, which in other services would have been inquired into by a court-martial, he was forthwith made a General, and shortly afterward called to the post of Chief of the Staff.

When Colin Campbell advanced to Lucknow, he left the old intrenchments, the camp and the town of Cawnpore, together with the bridge over the Ganges, in charge of General Windham and a force sufficient for the purpose. There were five regiments of infantry, whole or in part, many guns of position, 10 field guns and two naval guns, besides 100 horse; the whole force above 2,000. While Campbell was engaged at Lucknow, the various bodies of rebels hovering about the Doab drew together for an attack on Cawnpore. Besides a miscellaneous rabble, collected by insurgent zemindars, the attacking force counted, of drilled troops (disciplined they cannot be called), the remainder of the Dinapur sepoys and a portion of the Gwalior contingent. These latter were the only insurgent troops, the formation of which can be said to go beyond that of companies, as they had been officered by natives almost exclusively, and thus, with their field officers and captains, retained something like organized battalions. They were consequently regarded with some respect by the British. Windham had strict orders to remain on the defensive, but getting no replies to his dispatches from Campbell, the communication being interrupted, he resolved to act on his own responsibility. On the 26th November, he advanced with 1,200 infantry, 100 horse and 8 guns to meet the advancing insurgents. Having easily defeated their vanguard, he saw the main column approaching and retired close to Cawnpore. Here he took up a position in front of the town, the 34th Regiment on the left, the rifles (5 companies) and two companies of the 82d on the right. The line of retreat lay through the town, and there were some brick-kilns in rear of the left. Within four hundred yards from the front, and on various points still nearer to the flanks, were woods and jungle, offering excellent shelter to the advancing enemy. In fact, a worse position could not well have been chosen —the British exposed in the open plain, while the Indians could approach under shelter to within three or four hundred yards! To bring out Windham's "heroism" in a still stronger light, there was a very decent position close by, with a plain in front and rear, and with the canal as an obstacle before the front; but, of course, the worse position was insisted on. On the 27th November, the enemy opened a cannonade, bringing up his guns to the edge of the cover afforded by the jungle. Windham, who, with the modesty inherent in a hero, calls this a "bombardment", says his troops stood it for five hours; but after this time, there happened something which neither Windham, nor any man present, nor any Indian or British newspaper, has as yet dared to relate. From the moment the cannonade was turned into a battle, all our direct sources of information cease, and we are left to draw our own conclusions from the hesitating, prevaricating and incomplete evidence before us. Windham confines himself to the following incoherent statement:

> "In spite of the heavy bombardment of the enemy, my troops resisted the attack [rather novel to call a cannonade against field troops an *attack*] for five hours, and still held the ground, until I found from the number of men bayoneted by the 88th, that the mutineers had fully penetrated the town; *having been told* that they were attacking the fort, I directed Gen. Dupuis to fall back. The whole force retired into the fort, with all our stores and guns, shortly before dark. Owing to the flight of the camp followers, I was unable to carry off my camp equipage and some of the baggage. Had not an error occurred in the conveyance of an order issued by me, I am of opinion that I could have held by ground, at all events until dark."

Gen. Windham, with that instinct shown already at the Redan, moves off to the reserve (the 88th occupying the town, as we must conclude), and finds, not the enemy alive and fighting, but a great number of the enemy bayoneted by the 88th. This fact leads him to the conclusion that the enemy (he does not say whether dead or alive) has fully penetrated the town! Alarming as this conclusion is both to the reader and to himself, our hero does not stop here. He is told that the fort is attacked. A common general would have inquired into the truth of this story, which of course turned out to be false. Not so Windham. He orders a retreat, though his troops could have held the position at least until dark, had not an error been committed in the conveyance of one of Windham's orders! Thus, first you have Windham's heroic conclusion, that where there are many dead sepoys there must be many live ones; secondly, the false alarm respecting the attack on the fort; and thirdly, the error committed in the conveyance of an order; all of which mishaps combined made it possible for a very numerous rabble of natives to defeat the hero of the Redan and to beat the indomitable British pluck of his soldiers.

Another reporter, an officer present, says:

"I do not believe anyone can accurately describe the fight and retreat of this forenoon. A retreat was ordered. Her Majesty's 34th Foot being directed to fall back behind the brick-kiln, neither officers nor men knew where to find it! The news flew rapidly about the cantonments that our force was worsted and on the retreat and an overwhelming rush was made at the inner intrenchments, as resistless as the mass of water at the Falls of Niagara. Soldiers and Jacks, Europeans and natives, men, women and children, horses, camels and oxen, poured in countless numbers from 2 p.m. By nightfall the intrenched camp, with its motley assemblage of men and beasts, baggage, luggage, and ten thousand non-descript incumbrances, rivaled the chaos that existed before the fiat of creation went forth."

Finally, *The Times*'s Calcutta correspondent states that evidently the British suffered on the 27th "what almost amounts to a repulse," but that from patriotic motives the Anglo-Indian press covers the disgrace with the impenetrable veil of charity. This much, however, is also admitted, that one of Her Majesty's regiments, composed mostly of recruits, one moment got into disorder, without however giving way, and that at the fort the confusion was extreme, Windham having lost all control over his men, until in the evening of the 28th Campbell arrived and "with a few haughty words" brought everybody to his place again.

Now, what are the evident conclusions from all these confused and prevaricating statements? No other than that, under the incapable direction of Windham, the British troops were completely, though quite unnecessarily, defeated; that when the retreat was ordered, the officers of the 34th Regiment, who had not even taken the trouble to get in any way acquainted with the ground they had fought on, could not find the place they were ordered to retreat to; that the regiment got into disorder and finally fled; that this led to a panic in the camp, which broke down all the bounds of order and discipline, and occasioned the loss of the camp equipage and part of the baggage; that finally, in spite of Windham's assertion about the stores, 15,000 Minié cartridges, the Paymaster's chests, and the shoes and clothing for many regiments and new levies, fell into the hands of the enemy.

English infantry, when in line or column, seldom run away. In common with the Russians, they have a natural cohesion which generally belongs to old soldiers only, and which is in part explained by the considerable admixture of old soldiers in both services, but it in part also evidently belongs to national character. This quality, which has nothing whatever to do with "pluck", but is on the contrary rather a peculiar development of the instinct of self-preservation, is still very valuable, especially in defensive positions. It also, in common with the phlegmatic nature of Englishmen, prevents panic; but it is to be remarked that when Irish troops are once disordered and brought to panic, they are not easy to rally. Thus it happened to Windham on Nov. 27. He will figure henceforth among that not very large but distinguished list of English generals who have succeeded in making their troops run away under a panic.

On the 28th the Gwalior contingent were reinforced by a considerable body from Bithur, and closed up to within four hundred yards of the British intrenched outposts. There was another engagement, conducted on the part of the assailants without any vigour whatever. During it an example of real pluck occurred on the part of the soldiers and officers of the 64th, which we are glad to relate, although the exploit itself was as foolish as the renowned Balaklava charge. The responsibility of it, too, is shifted upon a dead man—Col. Wilson of that regiment. It appears that Wilson advanced with one hundred and eighty men against four guns of the enemy, defended by far superior numbers. We are not told who they were; but the result leads to the conclusion that they were of the Gwalior troops. The British took the guns with a rush, spiked three of them, and held out for some time, when, no reinforcement arriving, they had to retreat, leaving sixty men and most of their officers on the ground. The proof of the hard fighting is in the loss. Here we have a small force, which, from the loss they suffered, must have been pretty well met, holding a battery till one-third of their numbers are down. This is hard fighting indeed, and the first instance of it we have since the storming of Delhi. The man who planned this advance, however, deserves to be tried by court-martial and shot. Windham says it was Wilson. He fell in it, and cannot reply.

In the evening the whole British force was pent up in the fort, where disorder continued to reign, and the position with the bridge was in evident danger. But then Campbell arrived. He restored order, drew over fresh troops in the morning, and so far repelled the enemy as to secure the bridge and fort. Then he made all his wounded, women, children and baggage cross, and held a defensive position until all these had a fair start on the road to Allahabad. As soon as this was accomplished, he attacked the sepoys on the 6th, and defeated them, his cavalry and artillery following them up for fourteen miles the same day. That there was little resistance offered is shown from

Campbell's report; he merely describes the advance of his own troops, never mentioning any resistance or manoeuvres on the part of the enemy; there was no check, and it was not a battle, but a *battue*. Brigadier Hope Grant, with a light division, followed the fugitives, and caught them on the 8th in the act of passing a river; thus brought to bay, they turned round and suffered severe loss. With this event Campbell's first campaign, that of Lucknow and Cawnpore, is brought to a close, and a fresh series of operations must begin, whose first developments we may expect to hear of within a fortnight or three weeks.

Written by F. Engels approximately on February 2, 1858.
Published in the *New-York Daily Tribune*, No. 5253 of February 20, 1858, as a leading article.

Printed according to the newspaper text

F. Engels

THE CAPTURE OF LUCKNOW[81]

The second critical period of the Indian insurrection has been brought to a close. The first found its centre in Delhi, and was ended by the storming of that city; the second centred in Lucknow, and that place, too, has now fallen. Unless fresh insurrections break out in places hitherto quiet, the revolt must now gradually subside into its concluding, chronic period, during which the insurgents will finally take the character of dacoits or robbers, and find the inhabitants of the country as much their enemies as the British themselves.

The details of the storming of Lucknow are not yet received, but the preliminary operations and the outlines of the final engagements are known. Our readers recollect that after the relief of the Residency of Lucknow, Gen. Campbell blew up that post, but left Gen. Outram with about 5,000 men in the Alambagh, an intrenched position a few miles from the city. He himself, with the remainder of his troops, marched back to Cawnpore, where Gen. Windham had been defeated by a body of rebels; these he completely beat, and drove them across the Jumna at Kalpi. He then awaited at Cawnpore the arrival of reinforcements and the heavy guns, arranged his plans of attack, gave orders for the concentration of the various columns destined to advance into Oudh, and especially turned Cawnpore into an intrenched camp of strength and proportions requisite for the immediate and principal base of operations against Lucknow. When all this was completed, he had another task to perform before he thought it safe to move —a task the attempting of which at once distinguishes him from almost all preceding Indian commanders. He would have no women loitering about the camp. He had had quite enough of the "heroines" at Lucknow, and on the march to Cawnpore; they had considered it quite natural that the movements of the army, as had always been the case in India, should be subordinate to their fancies and their comfort. No sooner had Campbell reached Cawnpore than he sent the whole interesting and troublesome community to Allahabad, out of his way; and immediately sent for the second batch of ladies, then at Agra. Not before they had reached Cawnpore, and not before he had seen them safely off to Allahabad, did he follow his advancing troops toward Lucknow.

The arrangements made for this campaign of Oudh were on a scale hitherto unprecedented in India. In the greatest expedition ever undertaken by the British there, the invasion of Afghanistan,[82] the troops employed never exceeded 20,000 at a time, and of these the great majority were natives. In this campaign of Oudh, the number of Europeans alone exceeded that of all the troops sent into Afghanistan. The main army, led by Sir Colin Campbell personally, consisted of three divisions of infantry, one of cavalry, and one of artillery and engineers. The first division of infantry, under Outram, held the Alambagh. It consisted of five European and one native regiment. The second (four European and one native regiment) and third (five European and one native regiment), the cavalry division under Sir Hope Grant (three European and four or five native regiments) and the mass of the artillery (forty-eight field guns, siege-trains and engineers), formed Campbell's active force, with which he advanced on the road from Cawnpore. A brigade concentrated under Brigadier Franks at Jaunpur and Azamgarh, between the Gumti and the Ganges, was to advance along the course of the former river to Lucknow. This brigade numbered three European regiments and two batteries, besides native troops, and was to form Campbell's right wing. Including it, Campbell's force in all amounted to —

	Infantry	Cavalry	Artillery and Eng'rs	Total
Europeans	15,000	2,000	3,000	20,000
Natives	5,000	3,000	2,000	10,000

or in all 30,000 men; to whom must be added the 10,000 Nepalese Gurkhas advancing under Jang Bahadur from Gorakhpur on Sultanpur, making the total of the invading army 40,000 men, almost all regular troops. But this is not all. On the south of Cawnpore, Sir H. Rose was advancing with a strong column from Sagar upon Kalpi and the Lower Jumna, there to intercept any fugitives that might escape between the two columns of Franks and Campbell. On the north-west, Brigadier Chamberlain crossed toward the end of February the Upper Ganges, entering the Rohilkhand, situated north-north-west of Oudh, and, as was correctly anticipated, the chief point of retreat of the insurgent army. The garrisons of the towns surrounding Oudh must also be included in the force directly or indirectly employed against that Kingdom, so that the whole of this force is certainly from 70,000 to 80,000 combatants, of which, according to the official statements, at least 28,000 are British. In this is not included the mass of Sir John Lawrence's force, which occupies at Delhi a sort of flank position, and which consists of 5,500 Europeans at Meerut and Delhi, and some 20,000 or 30,000 natives of the Punjab.

The concentration of this immense force is the result partly of Gen. Campbell's combinations, but partly also of the suppression of the revolt in various parts of Hindustan, in consequence of which the troops naturally concentrated toward the scene of action. No doubt Campbell would have ventured to act with a smaller force; but while he was waiting for this, fresh resources were thrown, by circumstances, on his hands; and he was not the man to refuse to avail himself of them, even against so contemptible an enemy as he knew he would meet at Lucknow. And it must not be forgotten that, imposing as these numbers look, they still were spread over a space as large as France; and that at the decisive point at Lucknow he could only appear with about 20,000 Europeans, 10,000 Hindus, and 10,000 Gurkhas —the value of the last, under native command, being at least doubtful. This force, in its European components alone, was certainly more than enough to insure a speedy victory, but still its strength was not out of proportion to its task; and very likely Campbell desired to show the Oudhians, for once, a more formidable army of white faces than any people in India had ever seen before, as a sequel to an insurrection which had been based on the small number and wide dispersion of the Europeans over the country.

The force in Oudh consisted of the remnants of most of the

mutinous Bengal regiments and of native levies from the country itself. Of the former, there cannot have been more than 35,000 or 40,000 at the very outside. The sword, desertion and demoralization must have reduced this force, originally 80,000 strong, at least one-half; and what was left was disorganized, disheartened, badly appointed, and totally unfit to take the field. The new levies are variously stated at from 100,000 to 150,000 men; but what their numbers may have been is unimportant. Their arms were but in part firearms, of inferior construction; most of them carried arms for close encounter only—the kind of fighting they were least likely to meet with. The greater part of this force was at Lucknow, engaging Sir J. Outram's troops; but two columns were acting in the direction of Allahabad and Jaunpur.

The concentric movement upon Lucknow began about the middle of February. From the 15th to the 26th the main army and its immense train (60,000 camp followers alone) marched from Cawnpore upon the capital of Oudh, meeting with no resistance. The enemy, in the meantime, attacked Outram's position, without a chance of success, on February 21 and 24. On the 19th Franks advanced upon Sultanpur, defeated both columns of the insurgents in one day, and pursued them as well as the want of cavalry permitted. The two defeated columns having united, he beat them again on the 23d, with the loss of 20 guns and all their camp and baggage. Gen. Hope Grant, commanding the advanced guard of the main army, had also, during its forced march, detached himself from it, and making a point to the left had, on the 23d and 24th, destroyed two forts on the road from Lucknow to Rohilkhand.

On March 2 the main army was concentrated before the southern side of Lucknow. This side is protected by the canal, which had to be passed by Campbell in his previous attack on the city; behind this canal strong intrenchments had been thrown up. On the 3d, the British occupied the Dilkhoosha Park, with the storming of which the first attack also had commenced. On the 4th, Brig. Franks joined the main army, and now formed its right flank, his right supported by the River Gumti. Meantime, batteries against the enemy's intrenchments were erected, and two floating bridges were constructed, below the town, across the Gumti; and as soon as these were ready, Sir J. Outram, with his division of infantry, 1,400 horse and 30 guns, moved across to take position on the left, or north-eastern bank. From here he could enfilade a great part of the enemy's line along the canal, and many of the intrenched palaces to its rear; he also cut off the enemy's communications with the whole north-eastern part of Oudh. He met with considerable resistance on the 6th and 7th, but drove the enemy before him. On the 8th, he was again attacked, but with no better success. In the meantime, the batteries on the right bank had opened their fire; Outram's batteries, along the river-bank, took the position of the insurgents in flank and rear; and on the 9th the 2d Division, under Sir E. Lugard, stormed the Martinière, which, as our readers may recollect, is a college and park situated on the south side of the canal, at its junction with the Gumti, and opposite the Dilkhoosha. On the 10th, the Bank-House was breached and stormed, Outram advancing further up the river, and enfilading with his guns every successive position of the insurgents. On the 11th, two Highland regiments (42d and 93d) stormed the Queen's Palace, and Outram attacked and carried the stone bridges leading from the left bank of the river into the town. He then passed his troops across and joined in the attack against the next building in front. On March 13, another fortified building, the Imambarrah, was attacked, a sap being resorted to in order to construct the batteries under shelter; and on the following day, the breach being completed, this building was stormed. The enemy, flying to the Kaisarbagh, or King's Palace, was so hotly pursued that the British entered the place at the heels of the fugitives. A violent struggle ensued, but by 3 o'clock in the afternoon the palace was in the possession of the British. This seems to have brought matters to a crisis; at least, all spirit of resistance seems to have ceased, and Campbell at once took measures for the pursuit and interception of the fugitives. Brigadier Campbell, with one brigade of cavalry and some horse artillery, was sent to pursue them, while Grant took the other brigade round to Sitapur, on the road from Lucknow to Rohilkhand, in order to intercept them. While thus the portion of the garrison which took to flight was provided for, the infantry and artillery advanced further into the city, to clear it from those who still held out. From the 15th to the 19th, the fighting must have been mainly in the narrow streets of the town, the line of palaces and parks along the river having been previously carried; but on the 19th, the whole of the town was in Campbell's possession. About 50,000 insurgents are said to have fled, partly to Rohilkhand, partly toward the Doab and Bundelkhand. In this latter direction they had a chance of escaping, as Gen. Rose, with his column, was still sixty miles at least from the Jumna, and was said to have 30,000 insurgents in front of him. In the direction of Rohilkhand there was also a chance of their being able to concentrate again; Campbell would not be in a position to follow them very fast, while of the whereabouts of Chamberlain we know nothing, and the province is large enough to afford them shelter for a short time. The next feature of the insurrection, therefore, will most likely be the formation of two insurgent armies in Bundelkhand and Rohilkhand, the latter of which, however, may soon be destroyed by concentric marches of the Lucknow and Delhi armies.

The operations of Sir C. Campbell in this campaign, as far as we can now judge, were characterized by his usual prudence and vigour. The dispositions for his concentric march on Lucknow were excellent, and the arrangements for the attack appear to have taken advantage of every circumstance. The conduct of the insurgents, on the other hand, was as contemptible, if not more so, than before. The sight of the redcoats struck them everywhere with panic. Franks's column defeated twenty times its numbers, with scarcely a man lost; and though the telegrams talk of "stout resistance" and "hard fighting," as usual, the losses of the British appear, where they are mentioned, so ridiculously small that we fear there was no more heroism needed and no more laurels to be gathered this time at Lucknow than when the British got there before.

Written by F. Engels on April 15, 1858.
Published in the *New-York Daily Tribune*, No. 5312 of April 30, 1858, as a leading article.

Printed according to the newspaper text

F. Engels

*DETAILS OF THE ATTACK ON LUCKNOW

At last we are in possession of detailed accounts of the attack and fall of Lucknow. The principal sources of information, in a military point of view, the dispatches of Sir Colin Campbell, have not yet, indeed, been published; but the correspondence of the British press, and especially the letters of Mr. Russell in the London *Times*, the chief portions of which have been laid before our readers, are quite sufficient to give a general insight into the proceedings of the attacking party.

The conclusions we drew from the telegraphic news, as to the ignorance and cowardice displayed in the defence, are more than confirmed by the detailed accounts.* The works erected by the Hindus, formidable in appearance, were in reality of no greater consequence than the fiery dragons and grimacing faces painted by Chinese "braves" on their shields or on the walls of their cities. Every single work exhibited an apparently impregnable front, nothing but loopholed and embrasured walls and parapets, difficulties of access of every possible description, cannon and small arms bristling everywhere. But the flanks and rear of every position were completely neglected, a mutual support of the various works was never thought of, and even the ground between the works, as well as in front of them, had never been cleared, so that both front and flank attacks could be prepared without the knowledge of the defence, and could approach under perfect shelter to within a few yards from the parapet. It was just such a conglomerate of intrenchments as might be expected from a body of private sappers deprived of

* See this collection, pp. 120-22. —*Ed.*

their officers, and serving in an army where ignorance and indiscipline reigned supreme. The intrenchments of Lucknow are but a translation of the whole method of sepoy warfare into baked clay walls and earthen parapets. The mechanical portion of European tactics had been partially impressed upon their minds; they knew the manual and platoon drill well enough; they could also build a battery and loophole a wall; but how to combine the movements of companies and battalions in the defence of a position, or how to combine batteries and loopholed houses and walls, so as to form an intrenched camp capable of resistance—of this they were utterly ignorant. Thus, they weakened the solid masonry walls of their palaces by over-loopholing them, heaped tier upon tier of loopholes and embrasures, placed parapeted batteries on their roofs, and all this to no purpose whatever, because it could all be turned in the easiest possible manner. In the same way, knowing their tactical inferiority, they tried to make up for it by cramming every post as full of men as possible, to no other purpose than to give terrible effect to the British artillery and to render impossible all orderly and systematic defence as soon as the attacking columns fell upon this motley host from an unexpected direction. And when the British, by some accidental circumstance, were compelled to attack even the formidable front of the works, their construction was so faulty that they could be approached, breached and stormed almost without any risk. At the Imambarrah this was the case. Within a few yards from the building stood a pucka (sun-baked clay) wall. Up to this the British made a short sap (proof enough that the embrasures and loopholes on the higher part of the building had no plunging fire upon the ground immediately in front), and used this very wall as a breaching battery, prepared for them by the Hindus themselves! They brought up two 68-pounders (naval guns) behind this wall. The lightest 68-pounder in the British service weighs 87 cwt., without the carriage; but supposing even that an 8-inch gun for hollow shot only is alluded to, the lightest gun of that class weighs 50 cwt., and with the carriage at least three tons. That such guns could be brought up at all in such proximity to a palace several stories high, with a battery on the roof, shows a contempt of commanding positions and an ignorance of military engineering which no private sapper in any civilized army could be capable of.

Thus much for the science against which the British had to contend. As to courage and obstinacy, they were equally absent from the defence. From the Martinière to the Musabagh, on the part of the natives, there was but one grand and unanimous act of bolting, as soon as a column advanced to the attack. There is nothing in the whole series of engagements that can compare even with the massacre (for fight it can scarcely be called) in the Sikandarbagh during Campbell's relief of the Residency. No sooner do the attacking parties advance, than there is a general helter-skelter to the rear, and where there are but a few narrow exits so as to bring the crowded rabble to a stop, they fall pellmell, and without any resistance, under the volleys and bayonets of the advancing British. The "British bayonet" has done more execution in any one of these onslaughts on panic-stricken natives than in all the wars of the English in Europe and America put together. In the East, such bayonet-battles, where one party only is active and the other abjectly passive, are a regular occurrence in warfare; the Burmese stockades[83] in every case furnished an example. According to Mr. Russell's account, the chief loss suffered by the British was caused by Hindus cut off from retreat, and barricaded in the rooms of the palaces, whence they fired from the windows upon the officers in the courtyards and gardens.

In storming the Imambarrah and the Kaisarbagh, the bolting of the Hindus was so rapid, that the place was not taken, but simply marched into. The interesting scene, however, was now only commencing; for, as Mr. Russell blandly observes, the conquest of the Kaisarbagh on that day was so unexpected that there was no time to guard against indiscriminate plunder. A merry scene it must have been for a true, liberty-loving John Bull to see his British grenadiers helping themselves freely to the jewels, costly arms, clothes, and all the toggery of His Majesty of Oudh. The Sikhs, Gurkhas and camp followers were quite ready to imitate the example, and a scene of plunder and destruction followed which evidently surpassed even the descriptive talent of Mr. Russell. Every fresh step in advance was accompanied with plunder and devastation. The Kaisarbagh had fallen on the 14th; and half an hour after, discipline was at an end, and the officers had lost all command over their men. On the 17th, Gen. Campbell was obliged to establish patrols to check plundering, and to remain in inactivity "until the present licence ceases". The troops were evidently completely out of hand. On the 18th, we hear that there is a cessation of the *grosser* sort of plunder, but devastation is still going on freely. In the city, however, while the vanguard were fighting against the natives' fire from the houses, the rear-guard plundered and destroyed to their hearts' content. In the evening, there is another proclamation against plundering; strong parties of every regiment to go out and fetch in their own men, and to keep their camp followers at home; nobody to leave the camp except on duty. On the 20th, a recapitulation of the same orders. On the same day, two British "officers and gentlemen", Lieuts. Cape and Thackwell, "went into the city *looting*, and were murdered in a house"; and on the 26th, matters were still so bad that the most stringent orders were issued for the suppression of plunder and outrage; hourly roll-calls were instituted; all soldiers strictly forbidden to enter the city; camp followers, if found armed in the city, to be hanged; soldiers not to wear arms except on duty, and all non-combatants to be disarmed. To give due weight to these orders, a number of triangles for flogging were erected "at proper places".

This is indeed a pretty state of things in a civilized army in the nineteenth century; and if any other troops in the world had committed one-tenth of these excesses, how would the indignant British press brand them with infamy! But these are the deeds of the British army, and therefore we are told that such things are but the normal consequences of war. British officers and gentlemen are perfectly welcome to appropriate to themselves any silver spoons, jewelled bracelets, and other little memorials they may find about the scene of their glory; and if Campbell is compelled to disarm his own army in the midst of war, in order to stop wholesale robbery and violence, there may have been military reasons for the step; but surely nobody will begrudge these poor fellows a week's holiday and a little frolic after so many fatigues and privations.

The fact is, there is no army in Europe or America with so much brutality as the British. Plundering, violence, massacre — things that everywhere else are strictly and completely banished — are a time-honoured privilege, a vested right of the British soldier. The infamies committed for days together, after the storming of Badajoz and San Sebastian,[84] in the Peninsular war, are without a parallel in the annals of any other nation since the beginning of the French Revolution; and the medieval usage, proscribed everywhere else, of giving up to plunder a town taken by assault, is still the rule with the British. At Delhi imperious military considerations enforced an exception; but the army, though bought off by extra pay, grumbled, and now at Lucknow they have made up for what they missed at Delhi. For twelve days and nights there was no British army at Lucknow — nothing but a lawless, drunken, brutal rabble, dissolved into bands of robbers, far more lawless, violent and greedy than the sepoys who had just been driven out of the place. The sack of Lucknow in 1858 will remain an everlasting disgrace to the British military service.

If the reckless soldiery, in their civilizing and humanizing progress through India, could rob the natives of their personal property only, the British Government steps in immediately afterward and strips them of their real estate as well. Talk of the First French Revolution confiscating the lands of the nobles and the church! Talk of Louis Napoleon confiscating the property of the Orleans family! Here comes Lord Canning, a British nobleman, mild in language, manners and feelings, and confiscates, by order of his superior, Viscount Palmerston, the lands of a whole people, every rood, perch and acre, over an extent of ten thousand square miles.[85] A very nice bit of *loot* indeed for John Bull! And no sooner has Lord Ellenborough, in the name of the new Government, disapproved of this hitherto unexampled measure, than up rise *The Times* and a host of minor British papers to defend this wholesale robbery, and break a lance for the right of John Bull to confiscate everything he likes. But then, John is an exceptional being, and what is virtue in him, according to *The Times*, would be infamy in others.

Meanwhile — thanks to the complete dissolution of the British army for the purpose of plunder — the insurgents escaped, unpursued, into the open country. They concentrate in Rohilkhand, while a portion carry on petty warfare in Oudh, and other fugitives have taken the direction of Bundelkhand. At the same time, the hot weather and the rains are fast approaching; and it is hot to be expected that the season will be so uncommonly favourable to European constitutions as last year. Then, the mass of the European troops were more or less acclimated; this year, most of them are newly arrived. There is no doubt that a campaign in June, July and August will cost the British an immense number of lives, and what with the garrisons that have to be left in every conquered city, the active army will melt down very rapidly. Already are we informed that reinforcements of 1,000 men per month will scarcely keep up the army at its effective strength; and as to garrisons, Lucknow alone requires at least 8,000 men, over one-third of Campbell's army. The force organizing for the campaign of Rohilkhand will scarcely be stronger than this garrison of Lucknow. We are also informed that among the British officers the opinion is gaining ground that the guerrilla warfare which is sure to succeed the dispersion of the larger bodies of insurgents, will be far more harassing and destructive of life to the British than the present war with its battles and sieges. And, lastly, the Sikhs are beginning to talk in a way which bodes no good to the English. They feel that without their assistance the British would scarcely have been able to hold India, and that, had they joined the insurrection, Hindustan would certainly have been lost to England, at least, for a time. They say this loudly, and exaggerate it in their Eastern way. To them the English no longer appear as that superior race which beat them at Mudki, Ferozeshah and Aliwal.[86] From such a conviction to open hostility there is but a step with Eastern nations; a spark may kindle the blaze.

Altogether, the taking of Lucknow has no more put down the Indian insurrection than the taking of Delhi. This summer's campaign may produce such events that the British will have, next winter, to go substantially over the same ground again, and perhaps even to reconquer the Punjab. But in the best of cases, a long and harassing guerrilla warfare is before them — not an enviable thing for Europeans under an Indian sun.

Written by F. Engels on May 8, 1858.
Published in the *New-York Daily Tribune*, No. 5333 of May 25, 1858, as a leading article.

Printed according to the newspaper text

K. Marx

THE ANNEXATION OF OUDH[87]

About eighteen months ago, at Canton, the British Government propounded the novel doctrine in the law of nations that a state may commit hostilities on a large scale against a province of another state, without either declaring war or establishing a state of war against that other state. Now the same British Government, in the person of the Governor-General of India, Lord Canning, has made another forward move in its task of upsetting the existing law of nations. It has proclaimed that

> "the proprietary right in the soil of the Province of Oudh is confiscated to the British Government, which will dispose of that right in such manner as it may see fitting."[88]

When, after the fall of Warsaw in 1831,[89] the Russian Emperor* confiscated "the proprietary right in the soil" hitherto held by numerous Polish nobles, there was one unanimous outburst of indignation in the British press and Parliament. When, after the battle of Novara,[90] the Austrian Government did not confiscate, but merely sequestered, the estates of such Lombard noblemen as had taken an active part in the war of independence, that unanimous outburst of British indignation was repeated. And when, after the 2d December, 1851, Louis Napoleon confiscated the estates of the Orleans family, which, by the common law of France, ought to have been united to the public domain on the accession of Louis Philippe, but which had escaped that fate by a legal quibble, then British

* Nicholas I. —*Ed.*

indignation knew no bounds, and the London *Times* declared that by this act the very foundations of social order were upset, and that civil society could no longer exist. All this honest indignation has now been practically illustrated. England, by one stroke of the pen, has confiscated not only the estates of a few noblemen, or of a royal family, but the whole length and breadth of a kingdom[91] nearly as large as Ireland, "the inheritance of a whole people", as Lord Ellenborough himself terms it.

But let us hear what pretexts — grounds we cannot call them — Lord Canning, in the name of the British Government, sets forth for this unheard-of proceeding: First, "The army is in possession of Lucknow." Second, "The resistance, begun by a mutinous soldiery, has found support from the inhabitants of the city and of the province at large." Third, "They have been guilty of a great crime, and have subjected themselves to a just retribution." In plain English: Because the British army have got hold of Lucknow, the Government has the right to confiscate all the land in Oudh which they have not yet got hold of. Because the native soldiers in British pay have mutinied, the natives of Oudh, who were subjected to British rule by force, have not the right to rise for their national independence. In short, the people of Oudh have rebelled against the legitimate authority of the British Government, and the British Government now distinctly declares that rebellion is a sufficient ground for confiscation. Leaving, therefore, out of the question all the circumlocution of Lord Canning, the whole question turns upon the point that he assumes the British rule in Oudh to have been legitimately established.

Now, British rule in Oudh was established in the following manner: When, in 1856, Lord Dalhousie thought the moment for action had arrived, he concentrated an army at Cawnpore which, the King of Oudh* was told, was to serve as a corps of observation against Nepal. This army suddenly invaded the country, took possession of Lucknow, and took the King prisoner. He was urged to cede the country to the British, but in vain. He was then carried off to Calcutta, and the country was annexed to the territories of the East India Company. This treacherous invasion was based upon article 6 of the treaty of 1801, concluded by Lord Wellesley.[92] This treaty was the natural consequence of that concluded in 1798 by Sir John

* Wajid Ali Shah. —*Ed.*

Shore. According to the usual policy followed by the Anglo-Indian Government in their intercourse with native princes, this first treaty of 1798 was a treaty of offensive and defensive alliance on both sides. It secured to the East India Company a yearly subsidy of 76 lacs of rupees ($ 3,800,000); but by articles 12 and 13 the King was obliged to reduce the taxation of the country. As a matter of course, these two conditions, in open contradiction to each other, could not be fulfilled by the King at the same time. This result, looked for by the East India Company, gave rise to fresh complications, resulting in the treaty of 1801, by which a cession of territory had to make up for the alleged infractions of the former treaty; a cession of territory which, by the way, was at the time denounced in Parliament as a downright robbery, and would have brought Lord Wellesley before a Committee of Inquiry, but for the political influence then held by his family.

In consideration of this cession of territory, the East India Company, by article 3, undertook to defend the King's remaining territories against all foreign and domestic enemies; and by article 6 guaranteed the possession of these territories to him and his heirs and successors for ever. But this same article 6 contained also a pit-fall for the King, viz.: The King engaged that he would establish such a system of administration, to be carried into effect by his own officers, as should be conducive to the prosperity of his subjects, and be calculated to secure the lives and property of the inhabitants. Now, supposing the King of Oudh had broken this treaty; had not, by his government, secured the lives and property of the inhabitants (say by blowing them from the cannon's mouth, and confiscating the whole of their lands), what remedy remained to the East India Company? The King was, by the treaty, acknowledged as an independent sovereign, a free agent, one of the contracting parties. The East India Company, on declaring the treaty broken and thereby annulled, could have but two modes of action: either by negotiation, backed by pressure, they might have come to a new arrangement, or else they might have declared war against the King. But to invade his territory without declaration of war, to take him prisoner unawares, dethrone him and annex his territory, was an infraction not only of the treaty, but of every principle of the law of nations.

That the annexation of Oudh was not a sudden resolution of the British Government is proved by a curious fact. No sooner was Lord Palmerston, in 1830, Foreign Secretary, than he sent an order to the then Governor-General* to annex Oudh. The subordinate at that time declined to carry out the suggestion. The affair, however, came to the knowledge of the King of Oudh,** who availed himself of some pretext to send an embassy to London. In spite of all obstacles, the embassy succeeded in acquainting William IV, who was ignorant of the whole proceeding, with the danger which had menaced their country. The result was a violent scene between William IV and Palmerston, ending in a strict injunction to the latter never to repeat such *coups d'état* on pain of instant dismissal. It is important to recollect that the actual annexation of Oudh and the confiscation of all the landed property of the country took place when Palmerston was again in power. The papers relating to this first attempt at annexing Oudh, in 1831, were moved for, a few weeks ago, in the House of Commons, when Mr. Baillie, Secretary of the Board of Control, declared that these papers had disappeared.

Again, in 1837, when Palmerston, for the second time, was Foreign Secretary, and Lord Auckland Governor-General of India, the King of Oudh*** was compelled to make a fresh treaty with the East India Company. This treaty takes up article 6 of the one of 1801, because "it provides no remedy for the obligation contained in it" (to govern the country well); and it expressly provides, therefore, by article 7,

> "that the King of Oudh shall immediately take into consideration, in concert with the British Resident, the best means of remedying the defects in the police, and in the judicial and revenue administrations of his dominions; and that if his Majesty should neglect to attend to the advice and counsel of the British Government, and if gross and systematic oppression, anarchy and misrule should prevail within the Oudh dominions, such as seriously to endanger the public tranquillity, the British Government reserves to itself the right of appointing its own officers to the management of whatsoever portions of the Oudh territory, either to a small or great extent, in which such misrule shall have occurred, for so long a period as it may deem necessary; the surplus receipts in such case, after defraying all charges, to be paid into the King's Treasury, and a true and faithful account rendered to his Majesty of the receipts and expenditure."

By article 8, the treaty further provides:

> "That in case the Governor-General of India in Council should be compelled to resort to the exercise of the authority vested in him by article 7, he will endeavour so far as possible to maintain, with such improvements as they

* William Bentinck. —*Ed.*

** Nazir-ed-Din. —*Ed.*

*** Mohammed Ali Shah. —*Ed.*

may admit of, the native institutions and forms of administration within the assumed territories, so as to facilitate the restoration of these territories to the Sovereign of Oudh, when the proper period for such restoration shall arrive."

This treaty professes to be concluded between the Governor-General of British India in Council, on one hand, and the King of Oudh on the other. It was, as such, duly ratified, by both parties, and the ratifications were duly exchanged. But when it was submitted to the Board of Directors of the East India Company, it was annulled (April 10, 1838) as an infraction of the friendly relations between the Company and the King of Oudh, and an encroachment, on the part of the Governor-General, on the rights of that potentate. Palmerston had not asked the Company's leave to conclude the treaty, and he took no notice of their annulling resolution. Nor was the King of Oudh informed that the treaty had ever been cancelled. This is proved by Lord Dalhousie himself (minute Jan. 5, 1856):

"It is very probable that the King, in the course of the discussions which will take place with the Resident,* may refer to the treaty negotiated with his predecessor in 1837; the Resident is aware that the treaty was not continued in force, having been annulled by the Court of Directors as soon as it was received in England. The Resident is further aware that, although the King of Oudh was informed at the time that certain aggravating provisions of the treaty of 1837, respecting an increased military force, would not be carried into effect, the *entire abrogation of it was never communicated to his Majesty*. The effect of this reserve and want of full communication is felt to be embarrassing to-day. It is the more embarrassing that the cancelled instrument was still included in a volume of treaties which was published in 1845, by the authority of Government."

In the same minute, sec. 17, it is said:

"If the King should allude to the treaty of 1837, and should ask why, if further measures are necessary in relation to the administration of Oudh, the large powers which are given to the British Government by the said treaty should not now be put in force, his Majesty must be informed that the treaty has had no existence since it was communicated to the Court of Directors, by whom it was wholly annulled. His Majesty will be reminded that the Court of Lucknow was informed at the time that certain articles of the treaty of 1837, by which the payment of an additional military force was imposed upon the King, were to be set aside. It must be presumed that it was not thought necessary at that time to make any communication to his Majesty regarding those articles of the treaty which were not of immediate operation, and that the subsequent communication was inadvertently neglected."

But not only was this treaty inserted in the official collection of 1845, it was also officially adverted to as a subsisting treaty in

* James Outram. —*Ed.*

Lord Auckland's notification to the King of Oudh, dated July 8, 1839; in Lord Hardinge's (then Governor-General) remonstrance to the same King, of November 23, 1847, and in Col. Sleeman's (Resident at Lucknow) communication to Lord Dalhousie himself, of the 10th December, 1851. Now, why was Lord Dalhousie so eager to deny the validity of a treaty which all his predecessors, and even his own agents, had acknowledged to be in force in their communications with the King of Oudh? Solely because, by this treaty, whatever pretext the King might give for interference, that interference was limited to an assumption of government by British officers *in the name of the King of Oudh*, who was to receive the surplus revenue. That was the very opposite of what was wanted. Nothing short of annexation would do. This denying the validity of treaties which had formed the acknowledged base of intercourse for twenty years; this seizing violently upon independent territories in open infraction even of the acknowledged treaties; this final confiscation of every acre of land in the whole country; all these treacherous and brutal modes of proceeding of the British toward the natives of India are now beginning to avenge themselves, not only in India, but in England.

Written by K. Marx on May 14, 1858.
Published in the *New-York Daily Tribune*, No. 5336 of May 28, 1858, as a leading article.

Printed according to the newspaper text

K. Marx

*LORD CANNING'S PROCLAMATION AND LAND TENURE IN INDIA

Lord Canning's proclamation in relation to Oudh, some important documents[93] in reference to which we published on Saturday, has revived the discussion as to the land tenures of India — a subject upon which there have been great disputes and differences of opinion in times past, and misapprehensions in reference to which have led, so it is alleged, to very serious practical mistakes in the administration of those parts of India directly under British rule.[94] The great point in this controversy is, what is the exact position which the zemindars, talukdars or sirdars, so called, hold in the economical system of India? Are they properly to be considered as landed proprietors or as mere tax-gatherers?

It is agreed that in India, as in most Asiatic countries, the ultimate property in the soil vests the Government; but while one party to this controversy insists that the Government is to be looked upon as a soil proprietor, letting out the land on shares to the cultivators, the other side maintains that in substance the land in India is just as much private property as in any other country whatever — this alleged property in the Government being nothing more than the derivation of title from the sovereign, theoretically acknowledged in all countries, the codes of which are based on the feudal law and substantially acknowledged in all countries whatever in the power of the Government to levy taxes on the land to the extent of the needs of the Government, quite independent of all considerations, except as mere matter of policy, of the convenience of the owners.

Admitting, however, that the lands of India are private

property, held by as good and strong a private title as land elsewhere, who shall be regarded as the real owners? There are two parties for whom this claim has been set up. One of these parties is the class known as zemindars and talukdars, who have been considered to occupy a position similar to that of the landed nobility and gentry of Europe; to be, indeed, the real owners of the land, subject to a certain assessment due to the Government, and, as owners, to have the right of displacing at pleasure the actual cultivators, who, in this view of the case, are regarded as standing in the position of mere tenants at will, liable to any payment in the way of rent which the zemindars may see fit to impose. The view of the case which naturally fell in with English ideas, as to the importance and necessity of a landed gentry as the main pillar of the social fabric, was made the foundation of the famous landed settlement of Bengal[95] seventy years ago, under the Governor-Generalship of Lord Cornwallis — a settlement which still remains in force, but which, as it is maintained by many, wrought great injustice alike to the Government and to the actual cultivators. A more thorough study of the institutions of Hindustan, together with the inconveniences, both social and political, resulting from the Bengal settlement, has given currency to the opinion that by the original Hindu institutions, the property of the land was in the village corporations, in which resided the power of allotting it out to individuals for cultivation while the zemindars and talukdars were in their origin nothing but officers of the Government, appointed to look after, to collect, and to pay over to the prince the assessment due from the village.

This view has influenced to a considerable degree the settlement of the landed tenures and revenue made of late years in the Indian provinces, of which the direct administration has been assumed by the English. The exclusive proprietary rights claimed by the talukdars and zemindars have been regarded as originating in usurpations at once against the Government and the cultivators, and every effort has been made to get rid of them as an incubus on the real cultivators of the soil and the general improvement of the country. As, however, these middlemen, whatever the origin of their rights might be, could claim prescription in their favour, it was impossible not to recognize their claims as to a certain extent legal, however inconvenient, arbitrary and oppressive to the people. In Oudh, under the feeble reign of the native princes, these feudal landholders had gone very far in curtailing alike the claims of the Government and the rights of the cultivators; and when, upon the recent annexation of that Kingdom, this matter came under revision, the Commissioners charged with making the settlement soon got into a very acrimonious controversy with them as to the real extent of their rights. Hence resulted a state of discontent on their part which led them to make common cause with the revolted sepoys.

By those who incline to the policy above indicated — that of a system of village settlement — looking at the actual cultivators as invested with a proprietary right in the land, superior to that of the middlemen, through whom the Government receives its share of the landed produce — the proclamation of Lord Canning is defended as an advantage taken of the position in which the great body of the zemindars and talukdars of Oudh had placed themselves, to open a door for the introduction of much more extensive reforms than otherwise would have been practicable — the proprietary right confiscated by that proclamation being merely the zemindari or talukdari right, and affecting only a very small part of the population, and that by no means the actual cultivators.

Independently of any question of justice and humanity, the view taken on the other hand by the Derby Ministry of Lord Canning's proclamation, corresponds sufficiently well with the general principles which the Tory, or Conservative, party maintain on the sacredness of vested rights and the importance of upholding an aristocratic landed interest. In speaking of the landed interest at home, they always refer rather to the landlords and rent-receivers than to the rent-payers and to the actual cultivators; and it is, therefore, not surprising that they should regard the interests of the zemindars and talukdars, however few their actual number, as equivalent to the interests of the great body of the people.

Here indeed is none of the greatest inconveniences and difficulties in the government of India from England, that views of Indian questions are liable to be influenced by purely English prejudices or sentiments, applied to a state of society and a condition of things to which they have in fact very little real pertinency. The defence which Lord Canning makes in his dispatch, published to-day, of the policy of his proclamation against the objections of Sir James Outram, the Commissioner of Oudh, is very plausible, though it appears that he so far yielded to the representations of the Commissioner as to insert into the proclamation the modifying sentence, not contained in the original draft sent to England, and on which Lord Ellenborough's dispatch was based.[96]

Lord Canning's opinion as to the light in which the conduct of landholders of Oudh in joining in the rebellion ought to be viewed does not appear to differ much from that of Sir James Outram and Lord Ellenborough. He argues that they stand in a very different position not only from the mutinous sepoys, but from that of the inhabitants of rebellious districts in which the British rule had been longer established. He admits that they are entitled to be treated as persons having provocation for the course they took; but at the same time insists that they must be made to understand that rebellion cannot be resorted to without involving serious consequences to themselves. We shall soon learn what the effect of the issue of the proclamation has been, and whether Lord Canning or Sir James Outram was nearer right in his anticipation of its results.

Written by K. Marx on May 25, 1858.
Published in the *New-York Daily Tribune*, No. 5344 of June 7, 1858, as a leading article.

Printed according to the newspaper text

F. Engels

*THE REVOLT IN INDIA

In spite of the great military operations of the English in the capture first of Delhi and then of Lucknow, the successive headquarters of the sepoy rebellion, the pacification of India is yet very far from being accomplished. Indeed, it may be almost said that the real difficulty of the case is but just beginning to show itself. So long as the rebellious sepoys kept together in large masses, so long as it was a question of sieges and pitched battles on a great scale, the vast superiority of the English troops for such operations gave them every advantage. But with the new character which the war is now taking on, this advantage is likely to be in a great measure lost. The capture of Lucknow does not carry with it the submission of Oudh; nor would even the submission of Oudh carry with it the pacification of India. The whole Kingdom of Oudh bristles with fortresses of greater or less pretensions; and though perhaps none would long resist a regular attack, yet the capture of these forts one by one will not only be a very tedious process, but it will be attended with much greater proportional loss than operations against such great cities as Delhi and Lucknow.

But it is not alone the Kingdom of Oudh that requires to be conquered and pacified. The discomfited sepoys dislodged from Lucknow have scattered and fled in all directions. A great body of them have taken refuge in the hill districts of Rohilkhand to the north, which still remains entirely in possession of the rebels. Others fled into Gorakhpur on the east — which district, though it had been traversed by the British troops on their march to Lucknow, it has now become necessary to recover a second time. Many others have succeeded in penetrating southward into Bundelkhand.

Indeed, a controversy seems to have arisen as to the best method of proceeding, and whether it would not have been better to have first subdued all the outlying districts which might have afforded the rebels a shelter, before directing operations against their main body collected at Lucknow. Such is said to have been the scheme of operations preferred by the military; but it is difficult to see how, with the limited number of troops at the disposal of the English, those surrounding districts could have been so occupied as to exclude the fugitive sepoys, when finally dislodged from Lucknow, from entering into them, and, as in the case of Gorakhpur, making their reconquest necessary.

Since the capture of Lucknow, the main body of the rebels appear to have retired upon Bareilly. It is stated that Nana Sahib was there. Against this city and district, upward of a hundred miles north-west from Lucknow, it has been judged necessary to undertake a summer campaign, and at the latest accounts Sir Colin Campbell was himself marching thither.

Meanwhile, however, a guerrilla warfare seems to be spreading in various directions. While the troops are drawn off to the north, scattered parties of rebel soldiery are crossing the Ganges into the Doab, interrupting the communication with Calcutta, and by their ravages disabling the cultivators to pay their land-tax, or at least affording them an excuse for not doing so.

Even the capture of Bareilly, so far from operating to remedy those evils, will be likely, perhaps, to increase them. It is in this desultory warfare that the advantage of the sepoys lies. They can beat the English troops at marching to much the same extent that the English can beat them at fighting. An English column cannot move twenty miles a day; a sepoy force can move forty, and, if hard pushed, even sixty. It is this rapidity of movement which gives to the sepoy troops their chief value, and this, with their power of standing the climate and the comparative facility of feeding them, makes them indispensable in Indian warfare. The consumption of English troops in service, and especially in a summer campaign, is enormous. Already, the lack of men is severely felt. It may become necessary to chase the flying rebels from one end of India to the other. For that purpose, European troops would hardly answer, while the contact of the wandering rebels with the native regiments of Bombay and Madras, which have hitherto remained faithful, might lead to new revolts.

Even without any accession of new mutineers, there are still in the field not less than a hundred and fifty thousand armed men, while the unarmed population fail to afford the English either assistance or information.

Meanwhile, the deficiency of rain in Bengal threatens a famine — a calamity unknown within this century, though in former times, and even since the English occupation, the source of terrible sufferings.

Written by F. Engels at the end of May, 1858.
Published in the *New-York Daily Tribune*, No. 5351 of June 15, 1858, as a leading article.

Printed according to the newspaper text

F. Engels

*THE BRITISH ARMY IN INDIA

Our indiscreet friend, Mr. William Russell of the London *Times*, has recently been induced, by his love of the picturesque, to illustrate, for the second time, the sack of Lucknow, to a degree which other people will not think very flattering to the British character. It now appears that Delhi, too, was "looted" to a very considerable extent, and that besides the Kaisarbagh, the city of Lucknow generally contributed to reward the British soldier for his previous privations and heroic efforts. We quote from Mr. Russell:

> "There are companies which can boast of privates with thousands of pounds worth in their ranks. One man I heard of who complacently offered to lend an officer 'whatever sum he wanted if he wished to buy over the captain'. Others have remitted large sums to their friends. Ere this letter reaches England, many a diamond, emerald and delicate pearl will have told its tale in a very quiet, pleasant way, of the storm and sack of the Kaisarbagh. *It is as well that the fair wearers ... saw not how the glittering baubles were won, or the scenes in which the treasure was trove*.... Some of these officers have made, literally, *their fortunes*.... There are certain small caskets in battered uniform cases which contain estates *in Scotland and Ireland*, and snug fishing and shooting boxes in every game-haunted or salmon-frequented angle of the world."

This, then, accounts for the inactivity of the British army after the conquest of Lucknow. The fortnight devoted to plunder was well spent. Officers and soldiers went into the town poor and debt-ridden, and came out suddenly enriched. They were no longer the same men; yet they were expected to return to their former military duty, to submission, silent obedience, fatigue, privation and battle. But this is out of the question. The army, disbanded for the purpose of plunder, is changed for ever; no word of command, no prestige of the General, can make it again what it once was. Listen again to Mr. Russell:

"It is curious to observe how riches develop disease; how one's liver is affected by loot, and what tremendous ravages in one's family, among the nearest and dearest, can be caused by a few crystals of carbon.... The weight of the belt round the private's waist, full of rupees and gold mohurs, assures him that the vision [of a comfortable independency at home] can be realized, and it is no wonder he resents the 'fall in, then, fall in!' ... Two battles, two shares of prize-money, the plunder of two cities, and many pickings by the way, have made some of our men too rich for easy soldiering."

Accordingly, we hear that above 150 officers have sent in their resignations to Sir Colin Campbell — a very singular proceeding indeed in an army before the enemy, which in any other service would be followed up in twenty-four hours by cashiering and severest punishment otherwise, but which, we suppose, is considered in the British army as a very proper act for "an officer and a gentleman" who has suddenly made his fortune. As to the private soldiers, with them the proceeding is different. Loot engenders the desire for more; and if no more Indian treasures are at hand for the purpose, why not loot those of the British Government? Accordingly, says Mr. Russell:

"There has been a suspicious upsetting of two treasure tumbrils under a European guard, in which some few rupees were missing, and *paymasters exhibit a preference for natives in the discharge of the delicate duty of convoy*!"

Very good, indeed. The Hindu or Sikh is better disciplined, less thieving, less rapacious than that incomparable model of a warrior, the British soldier! But so far we have seen the individual Briton only employed. Let us now cast a glance at the British army, "looting" in its collective capacity:

"Every day adds to the prize property, and it is estimated that the sales will produce £600,000. *The town of Cawnpore is said to be full of the plunder of Lucknow*; and if the damage done to public buildings, the destruction of private property, the deterioration in value of houses and land, and the results of depopulation could be estimated, it would be found that *the capital of Oudh has sustained a loss of five or six million sterling*."

The Kalmuk hordes of Genghis Khan and Timur, falling upon a city like a swarm of locusts, and devouring everything that came in their way, must have been a blessing to a country, compared with the irruption of these Christian, civilized, chivalrous and gentle British soldiers. The former, at least, soon passed away on their erratic course; but these methodic Englishmen bring along with them their prize-agents, who convert loot into a system, who register the plunder, sell it by auction, and keep a sharp look-out that British heroism is not defrauded of a title of its reward. We shall watch with curiosity the capabilities of this army, relaxed as its discipline is by the effects of wholesale plunder, at a time when the fatigues of a hot weather campaign require the greatest stringency of discipline.

The Hindus must, however, by this time be still less fit for regular battle than they were at Lucknow, but that is not now the main question. It is far more important to know what shall be done if the insurgents, after a show of resistance, again shift the seat of war, say to Rajputana, which is far from being subdued. Sir Colin Campbell must leave garrisons everywhere; his field army has melted down to less than one-half of the force he had before Lucknow. If he is to occupy Rohilkhand what disposable strength will remain for the field? The hot weather is now upon him; in June the rains must have put a stop to active campaigning, and allowed the insurgents breathing time. The loss of European soldiers through sickness will have increased every day after the middle of April, when the weather became oppressive; and the young men imported into India last winter must succumb to the climate in far greater numbers than the seasoned Indian campaigners who last summer fought under Havelock and Wilson. Rohilkhand is no more the decisive point than Lucknow was, or Delhi. The insurrection, it is true, has lost most of its capacity for pitched battles; but it is far more formidable in its present scattered form, which compels the English to ruin their army by marching and exposure. Look at the many new centres of resistance. There is Rohilkhand, where the mass of the old sepoys are collected; there is northeastern Oudh beyond the Gogra, where the Oudhians have taken up position; there is Kalpi, which for the present serves as a point of concentration for the insurgents of Bundelkhand. We shall most likely hear in a few weeks, if not sooner, that both Bareilly and Kalpi have fallen. The former will be of little importance, inasmuch as it will serve to absorb nearly all, if not the whole of Campbell's disposable forces. Kalpi, menaced now by General Whitlock, who has led his column from Nagpur to Banda, in Bundelkhand, and by General Rose, who approaches from Jhansi, and has defeated the advanced guard of the Kalpi forces, will be a more important conquest; it will free Campbell's base of operations, Cawnpore, from the only danger menacing it, and thus perhaps enable him to recruit his field forces to some extent by troops set at liberty thereby. But it is very doubtful whether there will be enough to do more than to clear Oudh.

Thus, the strongest army England ever concentrated on one

point in India is again scattered in all directions, and has more work cut out than it can conveniently do. The ravages of the climate, during the summer's heat and rains, must be terrible; and whatever the moral superiority of the European over the Hindus, it is very doubtful whether the physical superiority of the Hindus in braving the heat and rains of an Indian summer will not again be the means of destroying the English forces. There are at present but few British troops on the road to India, and it is not intended to send out large reinforcements before July and August. Up to October and November, therefore, Campbell has but that one army, melting down rapidly as it is, to hold his own with. What if in the meantime the insurgent Hindus succeed in raising Rajputana and Mahratta country in rebellion? What if the Sikhs, of whom there are 80,000 in the British service, and who claim all the honour of the victories for themselves, and whose temper is not altogether favourable to the British, were to rise?

Altogether, one more winter's campaign, at least, appears to be in store for the British in India, and that cannot be carried on without another army from England.

Written by F. Engels approximately on June 4, 1858.
Published in the *New-York Daily Tribune*, No. 5361 of June 26, 1858, as a leading article.

Printed according to the newspaper text

K. Marx

*TAXES IN INDIA

According to the London journals, Indian stock and railway securities have of late been distinguished by a downward movement in that market, which is far from testifying to the genuineness of the sanguine convictions which John Bull likes to exhibit in regard to the state of the Indian guerrilla war; and which, at all events, indicates a stubborn distrust in the elasticity of Indian financial resources. As to the latter, two opposite views are propounded. On the one hand, it is affirmed that taxes in India are onerous and oppressive beyond those of any country in the world; that as a rule throughout most of the presidencies, and through those presidencies most where they have been longest under British rule, the cultivators, that is, the great body of the people of India, are in a condition of unmitigated impoverishment and dejection; that, consequently, Indian revenues have been stretched to their utmost possible limit, and Indian finances are therefore past recovery. A rather discomfortable opinion this at a period when, according to Mr. Gladstone, for some years to come, the extraordinary Indian expenditure alone will annually amount to about £ 20,000,000 sterling. On the other hand, it is asserted —the asseveration being made good by an array of statistical illustrations —that India is the least taxed country in the world; that, if expenditure is going on increasing, revenue may be increased too; and that it is an utter fallacy to imagine that the Indian people will not bear any new taxes. Mr. Bright, who may be considered the most arduous and influential representative of the "discomfortable" doctrine, made, on the occasion of the second reading of the new Government of India bill,[97] the following statement:

"The Indian Government had cost more to govern India than it was possible to extort from the population of India, although the Government had been by no means scrupulous either as to the taxes imposed, or as to the mode in which they had been levied. It cost more than £30,000,000 to govern India, for that was the gross revenue, and there was always a deficit, which had to be made up by loans borrowed at a high rate of interest. The Indian debt now amounted to £ 60,000,000, and was increasing; while the credit of the Government was falling, partly because they had not treated their creditors very honourably on one or two occasions, and now on account of the calamities which had recently happened in India. He had alluded to the gross revenue; but as that included the opium revenue, which was hardly a tax upon the people of India, he would take the taxation which really pressed upon them at £25,000,000. Now, let not this £ 25,000,000 be compared with the £60,000,000 that was raised in this country. Let the House recollect that in India it was possible to purchase twelve days' labour for the same amount of gold or silver that would be obtained in payment for one in England. This £25,000,000 expended in the purchase of labour in India would buy as much as an outlay of £300,000,000 would procure in England. He might be asked how much was the labour of an Indian worth? Well, if the labour of an Indian was only worth 2d. a day, it was clear that we could expect him to pay as much taxation as if it was worth 2s. We had 30,000,000 of population in Great Britain and Ireland; in India there were 150,000,000 inhabitants. We raised here £60,000,000 sterling of taxes; in India, reckoning by the day's labour of the people of India, we raised £300,000,000 of revenue, or five times a greater revenue than was collected at home. Looking at the fact that the population of India was five times greater than that of the British Empire, a man might say that the taxation per head in India and England was about the same, and that therefore there was no great hardship inflicted. But in England there was an incalculable power of machinery and steam, of means of transit, and of everything that capital and human invention could bring to aid the industry of a people. In India there was nothing of the kind. They had scarcely a decent road throughout India."

Now, it must be admitted that there is something wrong in this method of comparing Indian taxes with British taxes. There is on the one side the Indian population, five times as great as the British one, and there is on the other side the Indian taxation amounting to half the British. But, then, Mr. Bright says, Indian labour is an equivalent for about one-twelfth only of British labour. Consequently £ 30,000,000 of taxes in India would represent £300,000,000 of taxes in Great Britain, instead of the £ 60,000,000 actually there raised. What then is the conclusion he ought to have arrived at? That the people of India in regard to their numerical strength pay the *same* taxation as the people in Great Britain, if allowance is made for the comparative poverty of the people in India, and £ 30,000,000 is supposed to weigh as heavily upon 150,000,000 Indians as £ 60,000,000 upon 30,000,000 Britons. Such being his supposition, it is certainly fallacious to turn round and say that a poor people cannot pay so much as a rich one, because the comparative poverty of the Indian people has already been taken into account in making out the statement that the Indian pays as much as the Briton. There might, in fact, another question be raised. It might be asked, whether a man who earns say 12 cents a day can be fairly expected to pay 1 cent with the same ease with which another, earning $ 12 a day, pays $ 1? Both would relatively contribute the same aliquot part of their income, but still the tax might bear in quite different proportions upon their respective necessities. Yet, Mr. Bright has not yet put the question in these terms, and, if he had, the comparison between the burden of taxation, borne by the British wage labourer on the one hand, and the British capitalist on the other, would perhaps have struck nearer home than the comparison between Indian and British taxation. Moreover, he admits himself that from the £ 30,000,000 of Indian taxes, the £ 5,000,000 constituting the opium revenue must be subtracted, since this is, properly speaking, no tax pressing upon the Indian people, but rather an export duty charged upon Chinese consumption. Then we are reminded by the apologists of the Anglo-Indian Administration that £ 16,000,000 of income is derived from the land revenue, or rent, which from times immemorial has belonged to the state in its capacity as supreme landlord, never constituted part of the private fortune of the cultivator, and does, in fact, no more enter into taxation, properly so called, than the rent paid by the British farmers to the British aristocracy can be said to enter British taxation. Indian taxation, according to this point of view, would stand thus:

Aggregate sum raised	£30,000,000
Deduct for opium revenue	£5,000,000
Deduct for rent of land	£16,000,000
Taxation proper	£9,000,000

Of this £ 9,000,000, again, it must be admitted that some important items, such as the post-office, the stamp duties, and the custom duties, bear in a very minute proportion on the mass of the people. Accordingly, Mr. Hendricks, in a paper recently laid before the British Statistical Society on the Finances of India, tries to prove, from parliamentary and other official documents, that of the total revenue paid by the people of India, not more than one-fifth is at present raised by taxation, i.e., from the real income of the people; that in Bengal 27 per cent only, in the Punjab 23 per cent only, in Madras 21 per cent only, in the north-western provinces 17 per cent only, and in Bombay 16 per cent only of the total revenue is derived from taxation proper.

The following comparative view of the average amount of taxation derived from each inhabitant of India and the United Kingdom, during the years 1855-56, is abstracted from Mr. Hendricks's statement:

Bengal, per head, revenue	£0 5 0	Taxation proper	£0 1 4
North-western provinces	3 5	Taxation proper	0 7
Madras	4 7	Taxation proper	1 0
Bombay	8 3	Taxation proper	1 4
Punjab	3 3	Taxation proper	0 9
United Kingdom	—	Taxation proper	1 10 0

For a different year the following estimate of the average paid by each individual to the national revenue is made by Gen. Briggs:

In England, 1852	£1 19 4
In France	1 12 0
In Prussia	19 3
In India, 1854	3 8½

From these statements it is inferred by the apologists of the British Administration that there is not a single country in Europe, where, even if the comparative poverty of India is taken into account, the people are so lightly taxed. Thus it seems that not only opinions with respect to Indian taxation are conflicting, but that the facts from which they purport to be drawn are themselves contradictory. On the one hand, we must admit the nominal amount of Indian taxation to be relatively small; but on the other, we might heap evidence upon evidence from parliamentary documents, as well as from the writings of the greatest authorities on Indian affairs, all proving beyond doubt that this apparently light taxation crushes the mass of the Indian people to the dust, and that its exaction necessitates a resort to such infamies as torture, for instance. But is any other proof wanted beyond the constant and rapid increase of the Indian debt and the accumulation of Indian deficits? It will certainly not be contended that the Indian Government prefers increasing debts and deficits because it shrinks from touching too roughly upon the resources of the people. It embarks in debt, because it sees no other way to make both ends meet. In

1805 the Indian debt amounted to £ 25,626,631; in 1829 it reached about £ 34,000,000; in 1850, £ 47,151,018; and at present it amounts to about £ 60,000,000. By the by, we leave out of the count the East Indian debt contracted in England, which is also chargeable upon the East Indian revenue.

The annual deficit, which in 1805 amounted to about two and a half millions, had, under Lord Dalhousie's Administration, reached the average of five millions. Mr. George Campbell of the Bengal Civil Service, and of a mind strongly biassed in favour of the Anglo-Indian Administration, was obliged to avow, in 1852, that:

> "Although no Oriental conquerors have ever obtained so complete an ascendancy, so quiet, universal and undisputed possession of India as we have, yet all have enriched themselves from the revenues of the country, and many have out of their abundance laid out considerable sums on works of public improvements.... From doing this we are de barred.... The quantity of the whole burden is by no means diminished [under the English rule], *yet we have no surplus*."

In estimating the burden of taxation, its nominal amount must not fall heavier into the balance than the method of raising it, and the manner of employing it. The former is detestable in India, and in the branch of the land-tax, for instance, wastes perhaps more produce than it gets. As to the application of the taxes, it will suffice to say that no part of them is returned to the people in works of public utility, more indispensable in Asiatic countries than anywhere else, and that, as Mr. Bright justly remarked, nowhere so extravagant is a provision made for the governing class itself.

Written by K. Marx on June 29, 1858. Published in the *New-York Daily Tribune*, No. 5383 of July 23, 1858, as a leading article.

Printed according to the newspaper text

F. Engels

THE INDIAN ARMY[98]

The war in India is gradually passing into that stage of desultory guerrilla warfare, to which, more than once, we have pointed* as its next impending and most dangerous phase of development. The insurgent armies, after their successive defeats in pitched battles, and in the defence of towns and intrenched camps, gradually dissolve into smaller bodies of from two to six or eight thousand men, acting, to a certain degree, independently of each other, but always ready to unite for a short expedition against any British detachment which may be surprised singly. The abandonment of Bareilly without a blow, after having drawn the active field force of Sir C. Campbell some eighty miles away from Lucknow, was the turning point, in this respect, for the main army of the insurgents; the abandonment of Kalpi had the same significance for the second great body of natives. In either case, the last defensible central base of operations was given up, and the warfare of an army thereby becoming impossible, the insurgents made eccentric retreats by separating into smaller bodies. These movable columns require no large town for a central base of operations. They can find means of existence, of re-equipment, and of recruitment in the various districts in which they move; and a small town or a large village as a centre of reorganization may be as valuable to each of them as Delhi, Lucknow or Kalpi to the larger armies. By this change, the war loses much of its interest; the movements of the various columns of insurgents cannot be followed up in detail and appear confused in the accounts; the

* See this collection, pp. 125-28, 139-41. — *Ed.*

operations of the British commanders, to a great extent, escape criticism, from the unavoidable obscurity enveloping the premises on which they are based; success or failure remain the only criterion, and they are certainly of all the most deceitful.

This uncertainty respecting the movements of the natives is already very great. After the taking of Lucknow, they retreated eccentrically — some south-east, some north-east, some north-west. The latter were the stronger body, and were followed by Campbell into Rohilkhand. They had concentrated and re-formed at Bareilly; but when the British came up, they abandoned the place without resistance, and again retreated in different directions. Particulars of these different lines of retreat are not known. We only know that a portion went toward the hills on the frontiers of Nepal, while one or more columns appear to have marched in the opposite direction, toward the Ganges and the Doab (the country between the Ganges and the Jumna). No sooner, however, had Campbell occupied Bareilly, than the insurgents, who had retreated in an easterly direction, effected a junction with some bodies on the Oudh frontier and fell upon Shahjahanpur, where a small British garrison had been left; while further insurgent columns were hastening in that direction. Fortunately for the garrison, Brigadier Jones arrived with reinforcements as early as the 11th of May, and defeated the natives; but they, too, were reinforced by the columns concentrating on Shahjahanpur, and again invested the town on the 15th. On this day, Campbell, leaving a garrison in Bareilly, marched to its relief; but it was not before the 24th of May that he attacked them and drove them back, the various columns of insurgents which had co-operated in this manoeuvre again dispersing in different directions.

While Campbell was thus engaged on the frontiers of Rohilkhand, Gen. Hope Grant marched his troops backward and forward in the South of Oudh, without any result, except losses to his own force by fatigue under an Indian summer's sun. The insurgents were too quick for him. They were everywhere but where he happened to look for them, and when he expected to find them in front, they had long since again gained his rear. Lower down the Ganges, Gen. Lugard was occupied with a chase after a similar shadow in the district between Dinapur, Jugdispore and Buxar. The natives kept him constantly on the move, and after drawing him away from Jugdispore, all at once fell upon the garrison of that place. Lugard returned, and a telegram reports his having gained a victory on the 26th. The identity of the tactics of these insurgents with those of the Oudh and Rohilkhand columns is evident. The victory gained by Lugard will, however, scarcely be of much importance. Such bands can afford to be beaten a good manytimes before they become demoralized and weak.

Thus, by the middle of May, the whole insurgent force of Northern India had given up warfare on a large scale, with the exception of the army of Kalpi. This force, in a comparatively short time, had organized in that town a complete centre of operations; they had provisions, powder and other stores in profusion, plenty of guns, and even foundries and musket manufactories. Though within 25 miles of Cawnpore, Campbell had left them unmolested; he merely observed them by a force on the Doab, or eastern side of the Jumna. Generals Rose and Whitlock had been on the march to Kalpi for a long while; at last Rose arrived, and defeated the insurgents in a series of engagements in front of Kalpi. The observing force on the other side of the Jumna, in the meantime, had shelled the town and fort, and suddenly the insurgents evacuated both, breaking up this, their last large army into independent columns. The roads taken by them are not at all clear, from the accounts received; we only know that some have gone into the Doab, and others toward Gwalior.

Thus the whole district from the Himalayas to the Bihar and Vindhya Mountains, and from Gwalior and Delhi to Gorakhpur and Dinapur, is swarming with active insurgent bands, organized to a certain degree by the experience of a twelve months' war, and encouraged, amid a number of defeats, by the indecisive character of each, and by the small advantages gained by the British. It is true, all their strongholds and centres of operations have been taken from them; the greater portion of their stores and artillery are lost; the important towns are all in the hands of their enemies. But on the other hand, the British, in all this vast district, hold nothing but the towns, and of the open country, nothing but the spot where their movable columns happen to stand; they are compelled to chase their nimble enemies without any hope of attaining them; and they are under the necessity of entering upon this harassing mode of warfare at the very deadliest season of the year. The native Indian can stand the midday heat of his summer with comparative comfort, while mere exposure to the rays of the sun is almost certain death to the European; he can march forty miles in such a season, where ten break down his northern opponent; to him even the hot rains and swampy jungles are comparatively innocuous, while dysentery, cholera, and ague follow every exertion made by Europeans in the rainy season or in swampy neighbourhoods. We are without detailed accounts of the sanitary condition of the British army; but from the comparative numbers of those struck by the sun and those hit by the enemy in Gen. Rose's army, from the report that the garrison of Lucknow is sickly, that the 38th Regiment arrived last autumn above 1,000 strong, now scarcely numbers 550, and from other indications we may draw the conclusion that the summer's heat, during April and May, has done its work among the newly-importated men and lads who have replaced the bronzed old Indian soldiers of last year's campaign. With the men Campbell has, he cannot undertake the forced marches of Havelock nor a siege during the rainy season like that of Delhi. And although the British Government are again sending off strong reinforcements, it is doubtful whether they will be sufficient to replace the wear and tear of this summer's campaign against an enemy who declines to fight the British except on terms most favourable to himself.

The insurgent warfare now begins to take the character of that of the Bedouins of Algeria against the French;[99] with the difference that the Hindus are far from being so fanatical, and that they are not a nation of horsemen. This latter is important in a flat country of immense extent. There are plenty of Mohammedans among them who would make good irregular cavalry; still the principal cavalry nations of India have not joined the insurrection so far. The strength of their army is in the infantry, and that arm being unfit to meet the English in the field, becomes a drag in guerrilla warfare in the plain; for in such a country the sinew of desultory warfare is irregular cavalry. How far this want may be remedied during the compulsory holiday the English will have to take during the rains, we shall see. This holiday will, altogether, give the natives an opportunity of reorganizing and recruiting their forces. Besides the organization of cavalry, there are two more points of importance. As soon as the cold weather sets in, guerrilla warfare alone will not do. Centres of operation, stores, artillery, intrenched camps or towns, are required to keep the British busy until the cold season is over; otherwise the guerrilla warfare might be extinguished before the next summer gives it fresh life. Gwalior appears to be, among others, a favourable point, if the insurgents have really got hold of it. Secondly, the fate of the insurrection is dependent upon its being able to expand. If the dispersed columns cannot manage to cross from Rohilkhand into Rajputana and the Mahratta country; if the movement remains confined to the northern central district, then, no doubt, the next winter will suffice to disperse the bands, and to turn them into dacoits, which will soon be more hateful to the inhabitants than even the pale-faced invaders.

Written by F. Engels on July 6, 1858. Published in the *New-York Daily Tribune*, No. 5381 of July 21, 1858, as a leading article.

Printed according to the newspaper text

K. Marx

THE INDIAN BILL[100]

The latest Indian bill has passed through its third reading in the House of Commons, and since the Lords, swayed by Derby's influence, are not likely to show fight, the doom of the East India Company appears to be sealed. They do not die like heroes, it must be confessed; but they have bartered away their power, as they crept into it, bit by bit, in a business-like way. In fact, their whole history is one of buying and selling. They commenced by buying sovereignty, and they have ended by selling it. *They have fallen*, not in a pitched battle, but under the hammer of the auctioneer, into the hands of the highest bidder. In 1693 they procured from the Crown a charter for twenty-one years by paying large sums to the Duke of Leeds and other public officers. In 1767 they prolonged their tenure of power for two years by the promise of annually paying £ 400,000 into the Imperial Exchequer. In 1769 they struck a similar bargain for five years; but soon after, in return for the Exchequer's foregoing the stipulated annual payment and lending them £ 1,400,000 at 4 per cent, they alienated some parcels of sovereignty, leaving to Parliament in the first instance the nomination of the Governor-General and four Councilors, altogether surrendering to the Crown the appointment of the Lord Chief Justice and his three Judges, and agreeing to the conversion of the Court of Proprietors from a democratic into an oligarchic body.[101] In 1858, after having solemnly pledged themselves to the Court of Proprietors to resist by all Constitutional "means" the transfer to the Crown of the governing powers of the East India Company, they have accepted that principle, and agreed to a bill penal as regards the Company, but securing emolument and place to its principal

Directors. If the death of a hero, as Schiller says, resembles the setting of the sun,* the exit of the East India Company bears more likeness to the compromise effected by a bankrupt with his creditors.

By this bill the principal functions of administration are intrusted to a Secretary of State in Council, just as at Calcutta the Governor-General in Council manages affairs. But both these functionaries — the Secretary of State in England and the Governor-General in India — are alike authorized to disregard the advice of their assessors and to act upon their own judgement. The new bill also invests the Secretary of State with all the powers at present exercised by the President of the Board of Control, through the agency of the Secret Committee — the power, that is, in urgent cases, of dispatching orders to India without stopping to ask the advice of his Council. In constituting that Council it has been found necessary, after all, to resort to the East India Company as the only practicable source of appointments to it other than nominations by the Crown. The elective members of the Council are to be elected by the Directors of the East India Company from among their own number.

Thus, after all, the name of the East India Company is to outlive its substance. At the last hour it was confessed by the Derby Cabinet that their bill contains no clause abolishing the East India Company, as represented by a Court of Directors, but that it becomes reduced to its ancient character of a company of stockholders, distributing the dividends guaranteed by different acts of legislation. Pitt's bill of 1784 virtually subjected their government to the sway of the Cabinet under the name of the Board of Control. The act of 1813 stripped them of their monopoly of commerce, save the trade with China. The act of 1834 destroyed their commercial character altogether, and the act of 1854 annihilated their last remnant of power, still leaving them in possession of the Indian Administration. By the rotation of history the East India Company, converted in 1612 into a joint-stock company, is again clothed in its primitive garb, only that it represents now a trading partnership without trade, and a joint-stock company which has no funds to administer, but only fixed dividends to draw.

The history of the Indian bill is marked by greater dramatic changes than any other act of modern parliamentary legislation.

---

* Schiller, *The Robbers*, Act III, Scene 2. —*Ed.*

When the sepoy insurrection broke out, the cry of Indian Reform rang through all classes of British society. Popular imagination was heated by the torture reports; the Government interference with the native religion was loudly denounced by Indian general officers and civilians of high standing; the rapacious annexation policy of Lord Dalhousie, the mere tool of Downing Street; the fermentation recklessly created in the Asiatic mind by the piratical wars in Persia and China —wars commenced and pursued on Palmerston's private dictation —the weak measures with which he met the outbreak, sailing ships being chosen for transport in preference to steam vessels, and the circuitous navigation around the Cape of Good Hope instead of transportation over the Isthmus of Suez —all these accumulated grievances burst into the cry for Indian Reform —reform of the Company's Indian Administration, reform of the Government's Indian policy. Palmerston caught at the popular cry, but resolved upon turning it to his exclusive profit. Because both the Government and the Company had miserably broken down, the Company was to be killed in sacrifice, and the Government to be rendered omnipotent. The power of the Company was to be simply transferred to the dictator of the day, pretending to represent the Crown as against the Parliament, and to represent Parliament as against the Crown, thus absorbing the privileges of the one and the other in his single person. With the Indian army at his back, the Indian Treasury at his command, and the Indian patronage in his pocket, Palmerston's position would have become impregnable.

His bill passed triumphantly through the first reading, but his career was cut short by the famous Conspiracy bill,[102] followed by the advent of the Tories to power.

On the very first day of their official reappearance on the Treasury benches, they declared that, out of deference for the decisive will of the Commons, they would forsake their opposition to the transfer from the Company to the Crown of the Indian Government. Lord Ellenborough's legislative abortion[103] seemed to hasten Palmerston's restoration, when Lord John Russell, in order to force the dictator into a compromise, stepped in, and saved the Government by proposing to proceed with the Indian bill by way of parliamentary resolution, instead of by a governmental bill. Then Lord Ellenborough's Oudh dispatch, his sudden resignation, and the consequent disorganization in the ministerial camp, were eagerly seized upon by Palmerston. The

Tories were again to be planted in the cold shade of opposition, after they had employed their short lease of power in breaking down the opposition of their own party against the confiscation of the East India Company. Yet it is sufficiently known how these fine calculations were baffled. Instead of rising on the ruins of the East India Company, Palmerston has been buried beneath them. During the whole of the Indian debates, the House seemed to indulge the peculiar satisfaction of humiliating the *Civis Romanus*.[104] All his amendments, great and small, were ignominiously lost; allusions of the most unsavory kind, relating to the Afghan war, the Persian war, and the Chinese war, were continually flung at his head; and Mr. Gladstone's clause, withdrawing from the Indian Minister the power of originating wars beyond the boundaries of India, intended as a general vote of censure on Palmerston's past foreign policy, was passed by a crushing majority, despite his furious resistance. But although the man has been thrown overboard, his principle, upon the whole, has been accepted. Although somewhat checked by the obstructive attributes of the Board of Council, which, in fact, is but the well-paid spectre of the old Court of Directors, the power of the executive has, by the formal annexation of India, been raised to such a degree that, to counterpoise it, democratic weight must be thrown into the parliamentary scale.

Written by K. Marx on July 9, 1858. Published in the *New-York Daily Tribune*, No. 5384 of July 24, 1858, as a leading article.

Printed according to the newspaper text

F. Engels

*THE REVOLT IN INDIA

The campaign in India has been almost completely suspended during the hot and rainy summer months. Sir Colin Campbell having secured, by a vigorous effort in the beginning of summer, all the important positions in Oudh and Rohilkhand, very wisely put his troops into quarters, leaving the open country in the possession of the insurgents, and limiting his efforts to maintaining his communications. The only episode of interest which occurred during this period in Oudh, was the excursion of Sir Hope Grant to Shahganj for the relief of Man Singh, a native chief, who, after a deal of tergiversation, had lately made his peace with the British, and was now blockaded by his late native allies. The excursion proved a mere military promenade, though it must have caused great loss to the British by sunstroke and cholera. The natives dispersed without showing fight, and Man Singh joined the British. The easy success of this expedition, though it cannot be taken as an indication of an equally easy subjection of the whole of Oudh, shows that the insurgents have lost heart completely. If it was the interest of the British to rest during the hot weather, it was the interest of the insurgents to disturb them as much as possible. But instead of organizing an active guerrilla warfare, intercepting the communications between the towns held by the enemy, of waylaying small parties, harassing the foragers, of rendering impassable the supply of victuals, without which no large town held by the British could live—instead of this, the natives have been satisfied with levying revenue and enjoying the leisure left to them by their opponents. Better still, they appear to have squabbled among themselves. Neither do they appear to have profited by the few quiet weeks to reorganize their forces, to refill their ammunition stores, or to replace the lost artillery. The bolt at Shahganj shows a still greater want of confidence in themselves and their leaders than any previous defeat. In the meantime, a secret correspondence is carried on between the majority of the chiefs and the British Government, who have after all found it rather impracticable to pocket the whole of the soil of Oudh, and are quite willing to let the former owners have it again on reasonable terms. Thus, as the final success of the British is now beyond all doubt, the insurrection in Oudh bids fair to die out without passing through a period of active guerrilla warfare. As soon as the majority of the landholders come to terms with the British, the insurgent bodies will be broken up, and those who have too much to fear from the Government will turn robbers (dacoits) in the capture of whom the peasantry will gladly assist.

South-west of Oudh the Jugdispore jungles appear to offer a centre for such dacoits. These impenetrable forests of bamboo and underwood are held by a party of insurgents under Amar Singh, who shows rather more activity and knowledge of guerrilla warfare; at all events, he attacks the British whenever he can, instead of quietly waiting for them. If, as is feared, part of the Oudh insurgents should join him before he can be expelled from his stronghold, the British may expect rather harder work than they have had of late. These jungles have now for nearly eight months served as a retreat to insurgent parties, who have been able to render very insecure the Grand Trunk Road from Calcutta to Allahabad, the main communication of the British.

In Western India, the Gwalior insurgents are still followed up by Gen. Roberts and Col. Holmes. At the time of the capture of Gwalior, it was a question of much consequence, what direction the retreating army might take; for the whole of the Mahratta country and part of Rajputana appeared ready for a rising as soon as a sufficiently strong body of regular troops arrived there to form a nucleus for the insurrection. A retreat of the Gwalior force in a south-westerly direction then seemed the most likely manoeuvre to realize such a result. But the insurgents, from reasons which we cannot guess at from the reports before us, have chosen a north-westerly direction. They went to Jaipur, thence turning south toward Udaipur, trying to gain the road to the Mahratta country. But this roundabout marching gave Roberts an opportunity of coming up with them, and defeating them totally without any great effort. The remnants of this body, without guns, without organization and ammunition, without leaders of repute, are not the men who are likely to induce fresh risings. On the contrary, the immense quantity of plunder which they carry along with them, and which hampers all their movements, appears already to have excited the avidity of the peasantry. Every straggling sepoy is killed and eased of his load of gold mohurs. If it has come to that, Gen. Roberts may safely leave the final dispersion of these sepoys to the country population. The loot of Sindhia's treasures by his troops saves the British from a renewal of the insurrection in a quarter more dangerous than Hindustan; for a rising in the Mahratta country would put the Bombay army upon a rather severe trial.

There is a fresh mutiny in the neighbourhood of Gwalior. A small vassal of Sindhia, Man Singh (not the Man Singh of Oudh) has joined the insurgents, and got hold of the small fortress of Paoree. This place is, however, already invested by the British, and must soon be captured.

In the meantime, the conquered districts are gradually pacified. The neighbourhood of Delhi, it is said, has been so completely tranquillized by Sir J. Lawrence that a European may travel about with perfect safety, unarmed, and without an escort. The secret of the matter is, that the people of every village have been made collectively responsible for any crime or outrage committed on its ground; that a military police has been organized; and, above all, that the summary justice of the court-martial, so peculiarly impressive upon Orientals, is everywhere in full swing. Still, this success appears to be the exception, as we do not hear anything of the kind from other districts. The complete pacification of Rohilkhand and Oudh, of Bundelkhand and many other large provinces, must yet require a very long time and give plenty of work yet to British troops and court-martials.

But while the insurrection of Hindustan dwindles down to dimensions which deprive it of almost all military interest, there has occurred an event far off, at the utmost frontiers of Afghanistan, which is big with the threat of future difficulties. A conspiracy to murder their officers and to rise against the British has been discovered among several Sikh regiments at Dera Ismael Khan. How far this conspiracy was ramified, we cannot tell. Perhaps it was merely a local affair, arising among a peculiar class of Sikhs; but we are not in a position to assert this. At all events, this is a highly dangerous symptom. There are now nearly 100,000 Sikhs in the British service, and we have heard how saucy they are; they fight, they say, to-day for the British, but may fight tomorrow against them, as it may please God. Brave, passionate, fickle, they are even more subject to sudden and unexpected impulses than other Orientals. If mutiny should break out in earnest among them, then would the British indeed have hard work to keep their own. The Sikhs were always the most formidable opponents of the British among the natives of India; they have formed a comparatively powerful empire; they are of a peculiar sect of Brahminism, and hate both Hindus and Mussulmans. They have seen the British "raj" in the utmost peril; they have contributed a great deal to restore it, and they are even convinced that their own share of the work was the decisive one. What is more natural than that they should harbour the idea that the time has come when the British raj shall be replaced by a Sikh raj, that a Sikh Emperor is to rule India from Delhi or Calcutta? It may be that this idea is still far from being matured among the Sikhs, it may be that they are so cleverly distributed that they are balanced by Europeans, so that any rising could be easily put down; but that this idea exists among them must be clear, we presume, to everybody who has read the accounts of the behaviour of the Sikhs after Delhi and Lucknow.

Still, for the present, the British have reconquered India. The great rebellion, stirred up by the mutiny of the Bengal army, is indeed, it appears, dying out. But this second conquest has not increased England's hold upon the mind of the Indian people. The cruelty of the retribution dealt out by the British troops, goaded on by exaggerated and false reports of the atrocities attributed to the natives, and the attempt at confiscating the Kingdom of Oudh, both wholesale and retail, have not created any particular fondness for the victors. On the contrary, they themselves confess that among both Hindus and Mussulmans, the hereditary hatred against the Christian intruder is more fierce than ever. Impotent as this hatred may be at present, it is not without its significance and importance, while that menacing cloud is resting over the Sikh Punjab. And this is not all. The two great Asiatic powers, England and Russia, have by this time got hold of one point between Siberia and India, where Russian and English interests must come into direct collision. That point is Peking. Thence westward a line will ere long be drawn across the breadth of the Asiatic continent, on which this collision of rival interests will constantly take place. Thus the time may indeed not be so very distant when "the sepoy and the Cossack will meet in the plains of the Oxus," and if that meeting is to take place, the anti-British passions of 150,000 native Indians will be a matter of serious consideration.

Written by F. Engels approximately on September 17, 1858.
Published in the *New-York Daily Tribune*, No. 5443 of October 1, 1858, as a leading article.

Printed according to the newspaper text

K. Marx

FROM "NOTES ON INDIAN HISTORY"

1856. Annexation of Oudh because of bad government on the part of the Nabob.—*Maharajah Dulip Singh of the Punjab adopted Christianity. Dalhousie* withdrew, leaving a *boastful "farewell minute"*; among other things, *canals, railways, electric telegraph* built; *increase in the revenue* of *£ 4 million* exclusive of annexation of Oudh; *tonnage of ships* trading to Calcutta, *nearly doubled*, in fact, *deficiency in the public accounts*, but this due to heavy expenditure for public works.—*Answer to this rodomontade*, the *Sepoy Revolution* (1857-59).

1857. The Sepoy Revolt. For some years *sepoy army* very disorganized; *40,000 soldiers from Oudh* in it, bound together by caste and nationality; one common pulse in army, insult to a regiment on the part of its superiors felt as grievance by all the rest; officers powerless; laxity of discipline; *open acts of mutiny frequent*, suppressed with more or less difficulty; *downright refusal of the Bengal army to cross the sea for the attack of Rangoon*,[105] necessitating the *substitution of Sikh regiments (1852)*. (All this since *annexation of Punjab*—1849—became worse *since annexation of Oudh—1856*.) *Lord Canning* began his administration with *arbitrary act;* until then, the *sepoys of Madras and Bombay enlisted* by regulation *for service all over the world*, the Bengalese only for *service in India; Canning* made *"general service enlistment"* the *rule in Bengal*. The "fakirs" denounced this as *attempt to abolish caste*, etc.

Early 1857. (Pam's) *cartridges, lately issued, greased with the fat of pigs and cows*, expressly, said the *fakirs*, in order to *cause every sepoy to break his caste.*

Hence, *sepoy émeutes* at *Barrackpore* (near Calcutta) and *Raniganj* (near *Bankura*).

February 26, sepoy émeute at *Berhampore* (*on the Hooghly*, south of *Murshidabad*); in *March*, sepoy insurrection at Barrackpore; all this in *Bengal* (forcibly quelled).

March and April. Sepoys of Ambala and Meerut set constantly and secretly *their barracks on fire*; in *districts of Oudh and north-west*, fakirs inflamed the people against England. *Nana Sahib*, *Rajah of Bithur* (on Ganges), plotted with *Russia*, *Persia*, *the princes of Delhi*, *ex-King of Oudh*, took advantage of the *sepoy disturbances* consequent upon the grease cartridges.

April 24. Rising at Lucknow of 48th Bengalese (Regiment), *3d Native Cavalry*, *7th Oudh Irregulars*, *quelled by Sir Henry Lawrence* bringing up English troops.

At Meerut (north-east of Delhi), *11th and 20th Native Infantry* attacked the English, shot their officers, fired the town, slew all English ladies and children, *went off to Delhi. At Delhi, in night, some of the mutineers* galloped into Delhi, *sepoys* there rose *(54th, 74th, 38th Native Infantry)*; *English Commissioner, chaplain, officers murdered*; 9 English officers defended the magazine, blew it up (2 perished); the other *Englishmen in the city* fled to jungles, most killed by natives or severe weather; some *arrived* safely at *Meerut*, now deserted of troops. But *Delhi in insurgent hands*.

At Ferozepore, 45th and 57th Native attempted to *seize the fort*, driven off by the *61st English*; but they plundered town, set it on fire, were next day driven off by cavalry turning off the fort.

At Lahore, on news of the events at Meerut and Delhi, *the sepoys on general parade*, ordered by General *Corbett disarmed* (surrounded *by English troops with artillery*).

May 20, 64th, 55th, 39th Native Infantry disarmed at *Peshawar* (as at Lahore); then the *remainder of available English and faithful Sikhs* cleared the beleaguered stations of *Naushahra and Mardan*, and *at the end of May*, the *large station of Ambala*, garrisoned by *several European regiments* assembled from the stations near; collected here, *nucleus of an army under General Anson*.... The *hill station of Simla*, crowded with English families resident there for the hot season, was *not attacked*.

May 25. Anson with his little army marched on *Delhi*; he *died* on *May 27*, replaced by *Sir Henry Barnard;* the latter on *June 7* joined by *English troops* under *General Wilson* (coming *from Meerut;* some fighting with the sepoys had taken place on the route).

Rebellion spread throughout Hindustan; in *20 different places simultaneously, sepoy risings and murder of the English;* chief scenes: *Agra, Bareilly, Moradabad. Sindhia* loyal to the "English dogs", not so his "*troopers*", *Rajah of Patiala*—for shame!—sent large body of soldiers in aid of the English.

At Mainpuri (north-western provinces), a young brute of a lieutenant, one *De Kantzow*, saved treasury and fort. *At Cawnpore, June 6, 1857, Nana Sahib* (had taken *command of 3 sepoy regiments* and *3 regiments of Native Cavalry*, who had risen at Cawnpore, while *Sir Hugh Wheeler*, commander of Cawnpore troops, had *only one battalion of [English] infantry*, and had obtained a *slight reinforcement* from without; he held the *fort and the barracks*, whither all English people, women, children had fled) *beleaguered Sir Hugh Wheeler.*

June 26, 1857. Nana Sahib offered safe retreat for all Europeans if *Cawnpore* delivered up; *June 27* (Wheeler having accepted), 400 of the survivors allowed to embark in boats and proceed down the Ganges; Nana opened fire on them from both sides; 1 boat escaped, attacked lower down, sunk, only 4 men of whole garrison escaped. *A boat*, which had stuck fast on a sandbank, filled with *women and children*, seized, marched to Cawnpore, there shut up closely as prisoners; *14 days later (in July)*, more English prisoners dragged there by the insurgent sepoys from *Fatehgarh* (military station 3 miles from *Farrukhabad). Upon orders from Canning*, troops moved from *Madras, Bombay, Ceylon.* On *May 23, Madras reinforcement* under *Neil* landed, and *Bombay contingent* up the *Indus*, proceeded to *Lahore.*

June 17. Sir Patrick Grant (succeeding *Anson* as *Commander-in-Chief in Bengal)* and *General Havelock*, the Adjutant General, *arrived at Calcutta*, started an once thence.

June 6, at Allahabad, sepoys mutinied, butchered the (English) *officers* with wives and children, attempted to *seize the fort*, defended by *Colonel Simpson*, who on *June 11* received aid from *Colonel Neill coming up with the Madras fusiliers from Calcutta;* the latter *turned out all*

Sikhs, occupied the fort, garrisoned the place only with Britishers. (On the way he had occupied *Benares* and defeated 37th Native Infantry in the first stage of mutiny; the *sepoys* fled); (English) *troops* flowed from all sides into Allahabad.

June 30. General *Havelock*, arriving at Allahabad, took command, marched with some 1,000 Britishers on *Cawnpore;* July 12, at *Fatehpur*, repulsed the sepoys, etc., *some more actions.*

July 16. Havelock s army on the outskirts of Cawnpore; defeated the Indians, but was too late *to enter the citadel; in the night, Nana butchered all English prisoners—officers, ladies, children;* then blew up the magazine and *abandoned the town.—July 17,* English troops entered the place.—*Hovelock* marched into Nana's nest, *Bithur*, took it unresisted, *destroyed the palace, blew up the fort,* then marched back to *Cawnpore;* there he left *Neill* to *garrison and hold the station,* while Havelock off *to relieve Lucknow;* there, despite the efforts of *Sir Henry Lawrence,* the whole city, *save the Residency,* fell into *insurgent hands.*

June 30. whole garrison marched out against body of rebels in vicinity; repulsed; *sheltered again in Residency;* this *place besieged.*

July 4. Sir Henry Lawrence died (consequent to *explosion of shell* wounding him on *July 2*); *Colonel Inglis took command;* they held out, with occasional sorties against the besiegers, *for three months.—Operations by Havelock* (p. 271).[106] After the latter back to *Cawnpore, Sir James Outram* joined him with large bodies of troops, and he ditto moved up reinforcements of *many detached regiments* from various mutinous districts.

September 19. the whole force crossed the Ganges under *Havelock, Outram, and Neill.* On 23d, they stormed the *Alambagh,* the *summer palace of the Kings of Oudh,* 8 miles from Lucknow.

September 25. final rush made on Lucknow, reached the *Residency,* where the united force had to stay, *closely blockaded, for 2 months more (General Neill* fell during the fighting in town; *Outram* received severe wound in arm.)

September 20. Delhi captured, after six days of actual fighting, under *General Wilson.* (Cf. pp. 272, 273 for details).

Hodson at the head of his body of horse broke into *palace*, seized *old King and Queen (Zinat Mahal)*; they were thrown in prison, while Hodson *with his own hand killed* (by shooting) *the princes. Delhi garrisoned and quieted.* Immediately after, *Colonel Greathead* went from Delhi to *Agra*, near which he defeated a *strong body of mutineers* from Holkar's capital, *Indore*.

October 10, he took *Agra*, then proceeded to Cawnpore, where he arrived on *October 26; meanwhile* mutineers defeated at Azamgarh, *Chattra* (near *Hazaribagh*), *Cajwa*, and in country round Delhi, under *Captain Boileau, Major English, Peel* (the latter with *naval brigade*; also, about to enter the scene of action, *Probyn's* and *Fane's Horse*, reinforcements from home; also, *regiments of volunteers* raised), and *Showers. Sir Colin Campbell* in *August* took command of Calcutta, prepared to carry war on larger scale.

November 19, 1857, Sir Colin Campbell delivered the besieged garrison in the *Residency at Lucknow, (Sir Henry Havelock died on November 24*); from *Lucknow*—

November 25, 1857—Colin Campbell proceeded to *Cawnpore*, which town had fallen into *insurgent hands* again.

December 6, 1857, Victorious battle by Colin Campbell before Cawnpore; the rebels fled, leaving the town deserted, were pursued and severely cut up by *Sir Hope Grant*. In *Patiala, Mainpuri*, rebels defeated by *Colonel Seaton, Major Hodson*, respectively; and in many other places.

January, 27, 1858, King of Delhi brought to court-martial under *Dawes*, etc.; sentenced to death as "felon" (representative of the Mogul dynasty, dating from 1526!); sentence commuted to *transportation for life to Rangoon. Conveyed* at end of the *year*.

Sir Colin Campbell's campaign of 1858. On *January 2, he took Farrukhabad* and *Fatehgarh*, established himself at *Cawnpore*, whither he ordered all available troops, stores, and guns from every quarter.—*Rebels were massed about Lucknow*, where *Sir James Outram* held them at bay.—After many other incidents (cf. pp. 276, 277), *Lucknow recaptured on March 15* (under Colin Campbell, *Sir James Outram, etc); looting* of the town, where *treasures of Oriental art stored up; fighting* over on *March 21*; last gun fired on *23d.—Flight of the insurgents to Bareilly*, headed by *Prince Firuz* [son of] Shah of *Delhi, Nana*

Sahib of Bithur, the *Moulavi of Fyzabad*, and *Hazrat Mahal*, the *Begum of Oudh*.

April 25, 1858. *Campbell* took *Shahjahanpur; Mogs* beat back attack by rebels *near Bareilly;* on *May 6, siege guns opened on Bareilly*, while *General Jones* came up by appointment after *having seized Moradabad; Nana* and his followers fled, *Bareilly taken without resistance. Shahjahanpur*, meanwhile closely invested by the rebels, relieved by *General Jones; Lugard's division*, marching from Lucknow, attacked, suffered severely at the hands of mutineers under *Kower Singh;* the *Moulavi of Fyzabad* killed soon afterwards, after *Sir Hope Grant* defeated the *Begum*, who fled to the *Gogra River* to rally new forces.

By mid-June 1858, mutineers defeated on all points; incapable of joint action; broken up into *bands of marauders* pressing hard the divided forces of the English. *Centres of action: the standards of the Begum*, the prince of Delhi and *Nana Sahib*.

Finishing stroke dealt to insurrection by Sir Hugh Rose's 2 months' (May and June) campaign in Central India.

January 1858, Rose took *Rahatgarh*, in *February*, *Sagar*, *and Garrakota*, marched on *Jhansi*, where the Ranee* had taken her stand.

April 1, 1858, severe action against *Tantia Topee*, cousin of *Nana Sahib*, who advanced from *Kalpi* to protect *Jhansi;* Tantia defeated.

April 4, Jhansi taken; the Ranee and Tantia Topee escaped, awaited the English at *Kalpi; while marching* thither—

May 7, 1858—Rose attacked by strong body of the enemy at the *town of Kunch;* he signally defeated them.

May 16, 1858, Rose within a few miles of Kalpi, closely invested the mutineers.

May 22, 1858, desperate *sortie* by the mutineers from Kalpi; they were worsted, fled.

May 23, 1858, Rose occupied Kalpi. Remained there few days for rest of his soldiers, who worn out [by campaign] hot summer.

June 2, young Sindhia (English dog-man) driven out of *Gwalior* by his troops after hard fighting, fled for his life to Agra. Rose marched on *Gwalior;* the *Ranee of Jhansi* and *Tantia Topee* at head of the rebels gave him—

---

* Lakshmi Bai. —*Ed.*

June 19—battle at the Loshkar Hill (before Gwalior); Ranee killed, her army dispersed after much slaughter, *Gwalior in English hands.*

During July, August, September 1858, Sir Colin Campbell, Sir Hope Grant, and General Walpole engaged to hunt down the more prominent rebels and take *all forts* whose possession disputed; *the Begum made some final stands,* then fled with *Nana Sahib across the Rapti River* to the territories of the English dog-man, *Jang Bahadur of Nepal;* he allowed the English to pursue the rebels into his country, thus the "last bands of desperadoes dispersed"; *Nana* and the *Begum fled into the hills,* while their followers laid down their arms.

Early 1859, Tantia Topee's hiding-place detected, he tried and executed.—*Nana Sahib* is "supposed" to have died in Nepal. *Khan of Bareilly* was seized and shot;
Mamu Khan of *Lucknow* sentenced to life imprisonment; others transported or imprisoned for various terms; *bulk of the rebels*—their regiments disbanded—laid down the sword, *became ryots.* The *Begum of Oudh* lived at Khatmandu in *Nepal.*

Confiscation of the soil of Oudh, which Canning declared to be property of the Anglo-Indian Government! Sir Robert Montgomery made *Chief Commissioner of Oudh* in place of Sir James Outram.

Abolition of the East India Company. It was broken even before the war at an end.

December 1857, Palmerston Indian Bill; first reading passed despite solemn protest by *the Board of Directors in February 1858,* but Liberal ministry replaced by Tory.

February 19, 1858, Disraeli's Indian Bill (cf. p. 281) fell through.

August 2, 1858, Lord Stanley's Indian Bill passed, and thereby *finis East India Co.* India a *province of the empire of the "great" Victoria!*

Written by K. Marx in the eighteen-seventies.

Printed according to the manuscript.
Translated from the German

CORRESPONDENCE

Marx to Engels

August 15, 1857

...It appears to me that in the affair with Delhi the English should begin their retreat as soon as the rainy season sets in in earnest. I risked on my own responsibility to forecast this,* since I had to deputize for you as military expert in the *Tribune*. N. B., on the supposition that the reports to date are true....

The persistent rumours of the fall of Delhi are being circulated by the Calcutta Government itself, and serve, as I see from the Indian papers, as the principal means of maintaining order in the Madras and Bombay presidencies. I am herewith sending you a plan of Delhi as a pastime, yet *you must send it back to me....*

---

* See this collection, pp. 49, 54, 56. —*Ed.*

Engels to Marx

Ryde, September 24, 1857

...Your wish about India coincided with the idea which occurred to me that you would probably like to hear my view about the whole business. At the same time, I found an opportunity to go through the main contents of the latest mail, map in hand, and *voici ce qui en résulte.*

The British positions in the Middle and Upper Ganges area are so terribly scattered that from the military standpoint the only right thing would be to join Havelock's troops and the Delhi contingent in Agra after they pick up as many as possible of the isolated and surrounded garrisons in that area; to hold Agra and just the neighbouring points *south* of the Ganges, and Gwalior (because of the Central Indian princes); to hold points situated down the Ganges, such as Allahabad, Benares and Dinapur, with local garrisons and reserves from Calcutta; in the meantime, to evacuate the women and the non-fighting population downriver, so as to make the troops efficient again, keep the environs in control by means of mobile units, and accumulate stocks. To retreat to Cawnpore if it is impossible to hold Agra, and even to Allahabad; this latter point, however, must be *defended to the last*, because it is the key to the country between the Ganges and the Jumna.

If Agra can be held and the Bombay army freely used, the Bombay and Madras armies should occupy the peninsula along the latitude of Ahmadabad and Calcutta and send columns to establish contact with the north —the Bombay army via Indore and Gwalior to Agra, and the Madras army via Sagar and Gwalior to Agra and via Jubbulpore to Allahabad. Other lines of communication to Agra run from the Punjab, provided the latter holds out, and from Calcutta via Dinapur and Allahabad. Thus there would be four communication lines and, save for the

Punjab, three lines of retreat—to Calcutta, Bombay and Madras. Concentrating troops from the south in Agra would help to subdue the Central Indian princes and quell the insurrection all along the line of march.

If Agra cannot be held, the Madras army must above all establish permanent communication lines with Allahabad and then withdraw with the Allahabad troops to Agra, while the Bombay army retreats to Gwalior.

The Madras army seems to have been recruited exclusively from riffraff and is therefore just so dependable. In Bombay they have 150 and more Indians to each battalion, and these are dangerous, because they can incite the others to mutiny. If the Bombay army mutinies, we shall have to give up all military forecasts for the time being; the only thing which is then certain is a colossal massacre from Cashmere to Cape Comorin. If the situation in Bombay is such that the army cannot be used against the insurgents, then, at least, the Madras columns, which have already advanced beyond Nagpur, must be reinforced and the earliest possible contact made with Allahabad or Benares.

The absurdity of the present British policy, caused by the complete absence of a truly supreme command, is coming to the surface chiefly in two mutually complementary things: firstly, in that by splitting their forces they are allowing themselves to be blocked in a multitude of small scattered posts, whereas, secondly, they are making their only mobile column dig in near Delhi, where it is not only incapable of doing anything, but is even coming to grief. The English general who ordered the march to Delhi should be court-martialled and hanged, for he ought to have known what we learned but recently, namely, that the British themselves had so reinforced the old defences that the city can be taken only in a regular siege by at least 15,000 to 20,000 men, and still many more if the stronghold is going to be *properly* defended. Now that they are there, they are compelled *to stay for political reasons*: a withdrawal would be tantamount to defeat, and yet they will scarcely be able to avoid it.

Havelock's troops have done very much. To traverse 126 miles in eight days and fight six or eight battles in such a climate and in such a season is beyond human endurance. But his troops are exhausted, so that he will also probably have to let himself be blocked after he exhausts his strength still more with expeditions over shorter distances round Cawnpore, or else he will have to return to Allahabad.

The real line of reconquest runs upwards along the Ganges Valley; Bengal proper is easier held, because its people have fallen terribly; it is near Dinapur that the really dangerous area begins. This is why Dinapur, Benares, Mirzapur, and especially Allahabad, are extremely important; from Allahabad the British could first conquer Doab (between the Ganges and Jumna) and the towns along the two rivers, then Oudh, and then the rest. The routes from Madras and Bombay to Agra and Allahabad can be just secondary operation routes.

The most important thing, as always, is concentration. The reinforcements sent up the Ganges are completely scattered. Not a single man has yet reached Allahabad. Perhaps this is inevitable, in order to consolidate these posts, or yet it is not. In any case the number of defended posts must be reduced to a minimum, because the forces must be concentrated for field operations. If C [olin] Campbell, about whom we so far only know that he is brave, wants to distinguish himself as a general, he must build up a mobile army *coûte que coûte, whether he abandons Delhi or not.* And wherever there are 25,000 to 30,000 European soldiers, the situation cannot be so desperate that he would fail to muster for a march at least 5,000 men, who would cover their losses with garrisons from other posts. Only *then* Campbell will see where he is and what kind of an adversary he essentially confronts. The odds are, however, that he *ira se blottir devant* Delhi like a fool, and will look on how his men die at the rate of 100 a day, and think it all the more "gallant" to stay where he is until they all die. Brave stupidity is still the order of the day.

Concentration of forces for a field war in the north, vigorous support of Madras and, if possible, Bombay — are all that is required. Even if the Mahratta princes along the bank of the Narbada fall away, this will mean nothing, if only for the fact that their troops are already with the insurgents. At any rate, the most that can be achieved is to hold out until the end of October, when new reinforcements arrive from Europe.

But if another couple of Bombay regiments mutiny, that will decide the entire issue, for tactics and strategy will fade out of the picture....

Engels to Marx

3, Edward Place, Jersey,
October 29, 1857

...The sepoys must have defended the *enceinte* of Delhi poorly; the big joke was the street fighting, in which the native troops were apparently sent ahead. The actual siege thus lasted from the 5th to the 14th; what followed was no longer a siege. This time was ample to knock breaches in the unprotected walls with heavy ship's guns from the distance of 300 to 400 yards which they had reached already by the 5th or 6th. The guns on the walls appear to have been poorly manned, or the English would not have managed to approach them so quickly....

Engels to Marx

December 31, 1857

Dear Moor,

I have looked all over the city for newspapers containing Indian news; I have sent you my "Guardians" the day before yesterday. I cannot get the numbers either at the *Guardian*,[107] or *The Examiner*[108] and *The Times*, and Belfield has no more. I thought you had finished the story Tuesday. In the circumstances, I cannot write the article, which annoys me all the more because this is the first afternoon in four weeks when I had the chance to write it without neglecting other urgent affairs. In future, let me know your intentions concerning military articles as early as possible. Just now twenty-four hours happens to be a lot of time for me.

In any case, information is terribly so scarce and everything is based on telegraphic dispatches from Cawnpore to Calcutta, that it is almost impossible to comment on them. The sole points are as follows. It is 40 miles from Cawnpore to Lucknow (Alambagh). Havelock's forced marches indicate that 15 miles is a very considerable march for India, involving much time. Accordingly, Colin* had just two or three marches before him and should at all events have come to Alambagh on the third day after leaving Cawnpore, with plenty of daylight still left to attack at once. It is by this that Colin's march is to be judged; I don't recall the dates. Secondly, he had about 7,000 men (it was thought that he had many more, but the march between Calcutta and Cawnpore must have been terribly bad and many men must have come to grief), and if he defeated the Oudhians

* Campbell. —*Ed.*

with about 7,000 men (inclusive of the garrisons of Alambagh and Lucknow), this was not a great feat. An army of 5,000-7,000 Englishmen has always been thought fully sufficient to go anywhere and do anything in the open field in India. That stamps the opponents at once. In this connection it should be borne in mind that the Oudhians, though the most warlike tribe in the Ganges Valley, are far below the sepoys in discipline, cohesion, armaments, etc., precisely because they have never been under direct European organization. Hence, the main battle was a running fight, that is to say, a skirmishing engagement in which the Oudhians were pushed back from post to post. Now, it is true, the British are, with the Russians, the worst light infantry in Europe, but they have learnt something in the Crimea, and at all events they had this great advantage over the Oudhians that their line of skirmishers was properly and regularly supported by pickets and lines, the whole under one individual commander and co-operating towards a single end; while their opponents in the normal Asiatic manner, dispersed in irregular clusters, everyone pressing to the front, thus offering a sixfold aim to the British, having no regular supports or reserves and each cluster commanded by its own clannish chief, acting independently of every other clan. For it must be repeated, up to now we have not heard in a single instance that any insurrectionary army in India had been properly constituted under a recognized chief. The dispatches gave no other indications about the nature of the battle. Furthermore, there is no description whatever of the terrain, and no details about the use of the troops, so that I can say absolutely nothing more (particularly from memory)....

Marx to Engels

January 14, 1858

...Your article is splendid in style and manner and reminiscent of the best days of the *Neue Rheinische Zeitung*.[109] As for Windham, he may be a very bad general, but this time the chap had the misfortune —which was his luck at Regan —of leading recruits into battle. I am generally of the opinion that this second army dedicated by the English to the Indians —and not a single man of it will return —can in no way match the first, which appears to have been wiped out almost entirely, in bravery, self-reliance and steadiness. As for the effect of the climate on the troops, I have shown by means of accurate calculations in various articles —so long as I ran the military department provisionally —that the death rate was disproportionately greater than the official English reports intimated. With the drain of men and bullion which it must cost the English, India is now our best ally....

Marx to Engels

April 9, 1859

...The Indian financial chaos should be viewed as the actual result of the Indian insurrection. A general breakdown appears inevitable, unless taxes are imposed on classes which have to date been England's most solid supporters. Yet essentially this is not going to be of great help. The joke is that John Bull will now have to pay 4 to 5 millions in cash in India vear after year to keep the machine going, and in this pretty roundabout way to raise his national debt again to the corresponding progressive ratio. Certainly, it is to be admitted that the Indian market for Manchester cottons is being paid for at a damned high price. According to the report of the Military Commission, 80,000 Europeans will have to be kept in India for many years alongside the 200,000 to 260,000 natives. This costs about £ 20 million, whereas the net revenue amounts to a mere £ 25 million. Furthermore, the insurrection has added a permanent debt of £ 50 million or, according to Wilson's estimate, a permanent annual deficit of 3 million. Moreover, the guarantee in railways of £ 2 million annually until they are put into operation, and a smaller sum permanently if their net revenue does not come up to 5 per cent. Until now, India (save the short stretch of railway which is ready) has had nothing from the affair but the honour of paying the English capitalists 5 per cent for their capital. But John Bull has cheated himself, or, rather, has been cheated by his own capitalists. India pays only nominally; it is John Bull who pays in fact. For example, a large part of Stanley's loan was made solely to pay the English capitalists 5 per cent for the railways they have not yet begun to build. Finally, the annual opium revenue of about £ 4 million received heretofore is much endangered by the Chinese treaty.[110] The monopoly is going to topple at all events, and the cultivation of opium in China itself is soon going to develop. The opium revenue rested precisely on the fact that it was an item of contraband. The current Indian financial catastrophe is, in my opinion, a grimmer affair than the Indian war has been....

NOTES

1 The article "The British Rule in India" was written by Marx in connection with the debates in the House of Commons concerning the renewal of the East India Company Charter. It was published in the *New-York Daily Tribune*.

The *New-York Daily Tribune* existed from 1841 to 1924. Founded by Horace Greeley, the prominent American journalist and politician, it was the organ of the Left-wing of the American Whigs until the mid-eighteen-fifties, and later of the Republican Party. In the forties and fifties it held progressive views and took a strong stand against slavery. A number of prominent American writers and journalists were associated with it. Charles Dana, who was strongly influenced by the ideas of utopian socialism, became one of its editors at the close of the eighteen-forties. Marx's association with the newspaper began in August 1851 and continued for more than ten years until March 1862. Many articles for the *New-York Daily Tribune* were written by Engels at Marx's request. The articles Marx and Engels wrote for the *New-York Daily Tribune* treated the key issues of international and domestic policy, the working-class movement, the economic development of the European countries, colonial expansion, the national-liberation movement in the oppressed and dependent countries, etc. During the period of reaction in Europe, Marx and Engels made broad use of the widely read American paper to expose with concrete materials the vices of capitalist society, its irreconcilable contradictions, and the limitations of bourgeois democracy.

In some cases the *New-York Daily Tribune* editors took considerable liberties with the articles contributed by Marx and Engels, publishing many of them unsigned in the form of editorials. There were also cases when they tampered with the text and dated the articles at will. Marx objected repeatedly against this. In connection with the economic crisis in the United States, which affected the finances of the newspaper, Marx was compelled to reduce the number of his articles in the autumn of 1857. Marx's association with the *New-York Daily Tribune* broke off entirely at the beginning of the American Civil War. This was largely due to the fact that advocates of a compromise with the slave-owning South had taken precedence in the newspaper and it departed from its former progressive positions. p. 13

2 By the *Turkish question* Marx meant the international antagonisms in the

Near East between the Great Powers vying for influence on the Ottoman Empire, particularly its Balkan possessions. This rivalry led ultimately to the Eastern, or Crimean, War of 1853-56 between Russia on the one hand and Britain, France, Turkey and Sardinia on the other. The crucial point of the Crimean War was the siege of Sevastopol, the Russian Black Sea naval base, which lasted eleven months and culminated in Sevastopol's surrender. But the vigorous and stubborn defence of Sevastopol by the Russian garrison weakened the Anglo-French-Turkish forces. They were no longer fit for offensive action. The war ended with the signing of the Peace Treaty of Paris in 1856.

The *Sardinian question* arose in 1853 when Austria broke off diplomatic relations with Piedmont (Sardinia) because the latter extended protection to participants of the national-liberation movement of 1848-49 and the Milan uprising of February 6, 1853, who had emigrated from Lombardy (then under Austrian rule).

By the *Swiss question* Marx meant the conflict which arose in 1853 between Austria and Switzerland over the stay in the Swiss canton of Tessin of participants of the Italian national-liberation movement, who had emigrated from districts in Italy then under Austrian rule, particularly Lombardy after the abortive uprising in Milan on February 6, 1853. p. 13

[3] The reference is to the debate in the Commons of a bill concerning a new Charter for the East India Company, the term of whose 1833 Charter had run out. The British East India Company, established in 1600, was an instrument of British colonial policy in India. The conquest of India, completed by the middle of the 19th century, was carried out by the British capitalists in the name of the Company, which from the first enjoyed a monopoly on trade with India and China. The Company also controlled and governed conquered territories in India, appointed civil servants and collected taxes. Its commercial and administrative privileges were defined in Charters periodically renewed by Parliament. In the 19th century the Company's commerce gradually lost in importance. An act of Parliament in 1813 deprived it of its commercial monopoly in India. It retained its monopoly solely on the tea trade and trade with China. Under the 1833 Charter the Company lost all its remaining commercial privileges, and the 1853 Charter somewhat curtailed the Company's monopoly on governing India. The East India Company was placed under a greater control of the British Crown. Its directors lost the right to appoint officials. The number of directors was reduced from 24 to 18, of whom six were appointed by the Crown. The President of the Board of Control was put on a par with the Secretary of State for India. Territorial control over the British possessions in India was retained by the Company until 1858, when it was finally abolished, and the government of India was placed directly under the Crown. p. 13

[4] *Court of Directors*—governing body of the East India Company elected annually from among the most influential associates of the Company and members of the British Government in India owning Company shares worth not less than £2,000. The Court of Directors had its seat in London and was elected by the general meeting of shareholders (Court of Proprietors), at which only holders of not less than £1,000 in shares had the right to vote. The Court had extensive powers in India until 1853. It was dissolved in 1858 when the East India Company was abolished. p. 13

[5] During the debate of a new Charter for the East India Company in the House of Commons in June 1853 Charles Wood, President of the Board of

Control, claimed that India was prospering. To prove his point he compared the contemporary situation in Delhi with the time when it was ravaged and destroyed by Nadir Shah (Kuli Khan), the Persian conqueror, in 1739. p. 14

6 The *Heptarchy* (government by seven rulers)—designation used in English historiography to denote the political system in England in the early Middle Ages, when the country was split into seven Anglo-Saxon kingdoms (6th-8th centuries); Marx uses this term by analogy to denote the feudal dismemberment of the Deccan before its conquest by the Moslems. p. 14

7 *Laissez faire, laissez aller*—formula of bourgeois Free Trade economists, advocates of free trade and non-interference by the state in economic relations. p. 15

8 Marx quotes an official House of Commons report published in 1812; the quotation is from G. Campbell's *Modern India: A Sketch of the System of Civil Government*, London, 1852, pp. 84-85. p. 17

9 *Glorious Revolution*—term used by English bourgeois historians to denote the *coup d'état* of 1688, which overthrew James II supported by the landed reactionary aristocracy and brought to power William III of Orange, who was connected with the major landowning manufacturers and top commercial interests. The 1688 coup extended the powers of Parliament, which gradually became the country's supreme governing body. p. 21

10 *Seven Years' War* (1756-63)—a war between two coalitions of European Powers—the Anglo-Prussian and the Franco-Russo-Austrian. One of the chief causes of the war was colonial and commercial rivalry between England and France. Aside from naval battles, hostilities between the latter two Powers unfolded chiefly in their American and Asian colonies. The main war theatre in the East was India, where the French and their vassal princes were opposed by the British East India Company, which had substantially increased its armed forces and took advantage of the war to seize a number of Indian territories. As a result of the Seven Years' War, France lost almost all its possessions in India (retaining control of only five coastal towns, whose defences it was obliged to demolish); England's colonial might was greatly strengthened. p. 21

11 J. Mill, *The History of the British India*. The first edition of this book appeared in 1818. Cited here is a passage from the 1858 edition, Vol. V, Book VI, pp. 60 and 65; the reference to the functions of the Board of Control, cited higher, is also from Mill's book (1858 ed., Vol. IV, Book V, p. 395) p. 22

12 *Anti-Jacobin War*—the war which England started against revolutionary France in 1793, when the Jacobins, a revolutionary democratic group, were in power in France, and which it continued against the Napoleonic Empire. p. 23

13 *Reform Bill* altered the method of sending members to the House of Commons; enacted in June 1832. The Reform Bill was aimed against the political monopoly of the landed and financial aristocracy and gave access to Parliament to representatives of the industrial bourgeoisie. The proletariat and the petty bourgeoisie, most prominent in the struggle for the reform, were duped by the liberal bourgeoisie and did not acquire electoral rights. p. 23

14 Marx lists a number of wars of conquest which the British East India Company waged in India with the purpose of seizing Indian territories and crushing its chief colonial rival—the French East India Company.

The *War in the Carnatic* lasted at intervals from 1746 to 1763. The warring sides—the British and French colonialists—sought to subjugate the Carnatic under the guise of supporting different local pretenders to the principality. The English, who in January 1761 took possession of Pondicherry, the principal French bastion in the south of India, ultimately won out.

In 1756, in an effort to avert a British invasion the nabob of Bengal started a war, seizing Calcutta, the British supporting base in north-eastern India. But the armed forces of the East India Company under Clive's command soon recaptured that city, demolished the French fortification in Bengal and defeated the nabob at Plassey on June 23, 1757. The uprising that broke out in 1763 in Bengal, which had been turned into a vassal possession of the Company, was crushed. Along with Bengal, the English took possession of Bihar, which was under the rule of the nabob of Bengal. In 1803, the English completed the conquest of Orissa, which embraced several local feudal principalities subjugated by the Company.

In 1790-92 and 1799 the East India Company waged wars against Mysore, whose ruler Tippoo Sahib had taken part in previous Mysore campaigns against the English and who was an implacable enemy of British colonialism. In the first of these wars Mysore lost half of its dominions, seized by the Company and its allied feudal princes. The second war culminated in a total defeat for Mysore and the death of Tippoo. Mysore became a vassal principality.

Subsidiary system, or the system of so-called *subsidiary agreements*, was a method of turning the potentates of Indian principalities into vassals of the East India Company. Most widespread were agreements under which the princes had to maintain (subsidize) the Company's troops stationed on their territory and agreements which saddled the princes with loans on exorbitant terms. Failure to fulfil them led to the confiscation of their possessions. p. 23

15 The first Anglo-Afghan War of 1838-42, started by the British with the aim of seizing Afghanistan, ended in total failure for the British colonialists.

The British colonialists seized *Scinde* in 1843. During the Anglo-Afghan War of 1838-42 the East India Company resorted to threats and violence to obtain the consent of the feudal rulers of Scinde for the passage of British troops across their possessions. Taking advantage of this the British demanded in 1843 that the local feudal princes proclaim themselves to be vassals of the Company. After crushing the rebel Beluchi tribes, the annexation of the entire region by British India was announced.

Punjab was conquered in British campaigns against the Sikhs in 1845-46 and 1848-49. The Sikh teaching of equality (their effort to reconcile Hinduism and Islam) became the ideology of the peasant movement against the Indian feudals and Afghan invaders in the late 17th century. As time went on, a feudal group emerged from among the Sikhs whose representatives stood at the helm of the Sikh state. In the early 19th century the latter included all Punjab and a number of neighbouring regions. In 1845, the British colonialists enlisted the support of traitors among the Sikh gentry to provoke a conflict with the Sikhs, and in 1846 succeeded in turning the Sikh state into a vassal principality. In 1848 the Sikhs revolted, but were totally subjugated in 1849. With the conquest of Punjab all India became a British colony. p. 24

16 T. M. [un] *A Discourse of Trade, from England unto the East-Indies: Answering to Diverse Objections Which Are Usually Made Against the Same*. London, 1621. p. 24

17 [Josiah Child], *A Treatise Wherein Is Demonstrated I. That the East-India Trade Is the Most National of All Foreign Trades.* London, 1681. Published under the pseudonym of fijnatpi (Patriot). p. 25

18 [John Pollexfen], *England and East-India Inconsistent in Their Manufactures. Being an Answer to a Treatise, Entitled, An Eassay on the East-India Trade*, London, 1697. p. 25

19 The conquest of Burma was begun by the British colonialists early in the 19th century. In the first Burmese War of 1824-26 the troops of the East India Company seized the Province of Assam bordering on Bengal and the coastal districts of Arakan and Tenasserim. The second Burmese War (1852) culminated in the seizure by the English of the Province of Pegu. A new campaign against Burma was expected in 1853, since no peace treaty had been signed at the close of the second Burmese War, and the new Burmese King, who assumed power in February 1853, refused to recognise the seizure of Pegu. p. 27

20 J. Dickinson, *The Government of India under a Bureaucracy*, London-Manchester, 1853, p. 50. Published by the Indian Reform Society, issue VI. p. 28

21 In the middle of the 17th century the Mahrattas started an armed struggle against the foreign domination of the Mogul feudal lords, delivering a telling blow at the Empire of the Great Moguls and contributing to its collapse. An independent Mahratta state emerged from this struggle, whose feudal lords soon started out on a series of wars of conquest. Late in the 17th century the Mahratta state was weakened by internal feudal strife, but in the early 18th century there again took shape a strong confederation of Mahratta principalities headed by a peshwa. The Mahratta feudal lords competed with the Afghans for hegemony in India, and in 1661 suffered a crushing defeat. Bled heavily by the struggle for supremacy in India and the internal strife of their feudal lords, the Mahratta principalities fell prey to the East India Company, which subjugated them in the Mahratta War of 1803-05. p. 29

22 *The zemindari and ryotwari* systems—introduced by the British authorities in India in the late 18th and early 19th century. The zemindar, who under the Great Moguls retained the right of succession to land as long as he paid the government a fixed part of the revenue he collected from the oppressed peasantry, was made by the British Government the proprietor of the land under the 1793 Act on Permanent Zemindari, and thus became a class supporter of the British colonial authorities. As the British spread their rule over India the zemindari system was extended in somewhat amended form not only to Bengal, Bihar and Orissa, but also to some other regions such as the United and Central provinces and a part of Madras Province. In areas where the system was introduced, the ryots, who were previously equal members of peasant communities, became tenants of the zemindars. Under the ryotwari system, introduced early in the 19th century in the Madras and Bombay presidencies, the ryots were termed holders of government land obliged to pay a rent-tax on their holding, which the British Administration in India fixed arbitrarily. At the same time the ryots were termed peasant proprietors of the land they rented. As a result of this juridically contradictory land-tax system, the land-tax was fixed at so high a level that the peasants were unable to pay it. They found themselves in arrears, and their land gradually fell into the hands of profiteers and usurers. p. 30

23 J. Chapman, *The Cotton and Commerce of India, Considered in Relations*

to the Interests of Great Britain; with Remarks on Railway Communication in the Bombay Presidency, London, 1851, p. 91. p. 32

[24] G. Campbell, *Modern India: A Sketch of the System of Civil Government*, London, 1852, pp. 59-60. p. 32

[25] The title accords with the entry in Marx's notebook for 1857. p. 35

[26] The author refers to the overthrow of the King of Oudh and Oudh's annexation by the East India Company, effected in 1856 by the British authorities in violation of existing agreements. (See pp. 135-41 of this collection.) p. 35

[27] The author alludes to the Anglo-Persian War of 1856-57, which was one of the links in Britain's aggressive colonial policy in Asia in the mid-19th century. The attempt of the Persian rulers to seize the Principality of Herat served as a pretext for the war. Herat, the capital of the principality, a commercial crossroads and an important strategic point, was in the middle of the 19th century an apple of contention between Persia, which had the support of Russia in this issue, and Afghanistan, which was encouraged by Britain. The seizure by Persian troops of Herat in October 1856 was used by the British colonialists as a pretext for armed intervention with a view of subjugating both Afghanistan and Persia. Declaring war on Persia, they sent their troops to Herat. However, the national-liberation uprising of 1857-59, which broke out in India at the time, compelled Britain to conclude a hasty peace. In March 1857 Persia renounced all her claims to Herat under a peace treaty signed in Paris. In 1863 Herat was incorporated in the possessions of the Afghan Emir. p. 36

[28] Uprising of 1857-59—major national-liberation uprising of the Indian people against British rule. Preceded as it was by a number of armed clashes with the British colonialists, the uprising was precipitated by the general indignation of all sections of the Indian population with the brutal methods of colonial exploitation—the exorbitantly high tax burden, little short of total plunder of the Indian peasantry and the expropriation of some strata of feudals; the policy of annexing the remaining independent Indian territories; the system of torture to extort taxes and the colonial reign of terror; and gross disregard by the colonialists of the time-honoured traditions and customs of the people. The uprising broke out in the spring of 1857 (preparations for it began in the summer of 1856) among the sepoy regiments of the Bengal army, quartered in Northern India. (Sepoys were mercenary troops of the Anglo-Indian army recruited since the mid-18th century from the native population. They were used by the British invaders to conquer India and to maintain power in the conquered provinces.) The sepoys held the key strategic points in the area and controlled much of the artillery. For this reason, they became the military core of the uprising. Recruited chiefly among the higher Hindu castes (Brahmins, Rajputs, etc.) and the Moslems, the sepoy army reflected essentially the discontent of the Indian peasantry—which supplied the bulk of rank-and-file sepoys—and a portion of the feudal gentry of Northern India (particularly Oudh), with which the sepoy officers were closely linked. The popular uprising, aimed at overthrowing foreign rule, spread to large areas of Nothern and Central India—chiefly Delhi, Lucknow, Cawnpore, Rohilkhand, Central India and Bundelkhand. The peasantry and poor urban artisan population were the main motive force of the uprising, but leadership was in the hands of the feudals, almost all of whom betrayed it after the colonial authorities promised in

1858 to leave their possessions intact. The main reason for the defeat of the uprising was the lack of single leadership and a general plan of operations, owing largely to the feudal disunity of India, the ethnically heterogeneous population, and the religious and caste division of the Indian people. The English made the most of this. Furthermore, they had the assistance of the majority of Indian feudals in suppressing the uprising. The considerable military and technical superiority was another telling factor. Although the uprising did not directly involve some parts of the country (the English succeeded in preventing its spreading to the Punjab, Bengal and the south of India), it had an impact on all India and compelled the British authorities to reform the system of government in that country. Closely associated with the national-liberation movement in other Asian countries, the Indian uprising weakened the positions of the colonialists. In particular, it delayed for dozens of years their aggressive plans with regard to Afghanistan, Persia and a number of other Asian countries. p. 36

29 Reference is made to the so-called Second Opium War with China in 1856-58. The pretext for it was a trumped-up British conflict with the Chinese authorities in Canton in October 1856. The conflict was over the arrest by the Chinese authorities of the crew of the Chinese ship *Arrow*, which sailed under the British flag with an illicit cargo of opium. Hostilities in China continued at intervals until June 1858 and culminated in the predacious Tientsin Treaty. p. 36

30 The reference is to Fort William—the English Fortress in Calcutta, built in 1696 and named in honour of William III of Orange, King of England at that time. After the English conquered Bengal in 1757, government buildings were housed in the fortress and its name began to signify "the government of the Bengal presidency" and subsequently "the English government of India". p. 37

31 *The Times*—prominent English conservative daily newspaper. Founded in London in 1785. p. 40

32 The Peninsular War was fought in the Iberian Peninsula on the territory of Spain and Portugal by Britain and France in 1808-14. A simultaneous war broke out throughout the Peninsula, in which the Spanish and Portuguese peoples fought for their independence against the French occupation. The struggle of the Spanish people contributed greatly to the failure of Napoleon's political and military plans; the latter was compelled after his disaster in Russia in 1812 to withdraw his troops from Spain. p. 41

33 The author apparently alludes to the fact that members of the British House of Commons often prefer personal pursuits and recreation to their parliamentary duties during the summer sessions of Parliament. For this reason, speakers often have to address an almost empty auditorium. p. 43

34 The reference is to Montesquieu's *Considérations sur les causes de la grandeur des Romains et de leur décadence*, the first edition of which appeared anonymously in Amsterdam in 1734, and to Gibbon's *The History of the Decline and Fall of the Roman Empire*, the first edition of which appeared in London, in 1776-88. p. 44

35 The author refers to the Tories—the party of the big British landed and financial aristocracy. Founded in the 17th century the Tory Party has always advocated reactionary internal policies and stood persistently by all the conservative and archaic institutions of Britain's system of government. It

opposed all democratic changes. With the development of capitalism in Britain, the Tories gradually lost their former political influence and their monopoly in Parliament. The first blow at this monopoly was struck by the 1832 Reform, which opened the way to Parliament to representatives of the industrial bourgeoisie. The abolition in 1846 of the Corn Laws, beneficial to landowners, weakened the old British landed aristocracy economically and led to the split in the party. The mid-1850's witnessed a process of disintegration in the Tory Party. Its class composition changed, mirroring the integration of the landed aristocracy and the capitalist magnates. Thus, the British Conservative Party evolved from the old Tory Party in the late fifties and early sixties. p. 44

36 Until 1773 the East India Company had three governors in India—in Calcutta (Bengal), Madras and Bombay. Each had a Council of senior Company employees. The Regulating Act of 1773 established a Council of four under the Governor of Calcutta, who was titled Governor-General of Bengal. The Governor-General and his Council were no longer nominated by the Company, but, as a rule, by the British Government for a term of five years and could be dismissed before this term only by the King upon representations of the Court of Directors of the Company. The opinion of the majority was obligatory for the whole Council. If the vote broke even, the Governor-General's vote was decisive. The Governor-General was charged with the civil and military administration of Bengal, Bihar and Orissa, and also had supreme control over the presidencies of Madras and Bombay, which were subordinate to him in matters concerning war and peace. It was only in special cases that the latter could act on their own. Under the 1784 Act, the Bengal Council was reduced to three members, one of them being the Commander-in-Chief. Under a supplementary Act of 1786 the Governor-General was authorised in emergencies to act independently of his Council and to assume the functions of the Commander-in-Chief. Under the Act of 1833 the Governor-General of Bengal was made Governor-General of India, whilst remaining Governor of Bengal. This Council was again made a four-member body with the Commander-in-Chief as a possible fifth additional member. The Governor-General and his Council were authorised to make laws for all of British India. The governments of Bombay and Madras were deprived of this right. The councils of their governors were to consist of two men. Under the Act of 1853 the Council of four members with the functions of an executive body, was supplemented with a larger legislative council which included the Governor-General, the Commander-in-Chief, the Lord Chief Justice of Bengal and one of his three judges. This statute of the Governor-General in Council was in force until 1858.

The reference is to the Council under Governor-General Lord Dalhousie. p. 45

37 The title accords with an entry in Marx's notebook for 1857. p. 48

38 The *Board of Control* was instituted under the 1784 Act for the better government of the East India Company and Britain's Indian possessions. The Board of Control was composed of six members appointed by the King from among the members of the Privy Council. The President of the Board of Control was a member of the Cabinet, and, in effect, the Secretary of State for India and India's supreme ruler. The decisions of the Board of Control, which sat in London, were conveyed to India by the Secret Committee, which consisted of three East India Company directors. In this way the 1784 Act established a dual system of government in India—the Board of Control

(British Government) and the Court of Directors (East India Company). The Board of Control was dissolved in 1858. p. 48

39 Early in October 1854 a rumour was spread in Paris about the capture of Sevastopol by the allies. The hoax was picked up by the official press in France, Britain, Belgium, and Germany. However, a few days later, the French newspapers were compelled to deny the report. p. 51

40 *The Bombay Times*—daily English-language newspaper founded in Bombay in 1838. p. 51

41 *The Press*—Tory weekly, published in London from 1853 to 1866. p. 52

42 *Le Pays*—French daily founded in Paris in 1849. At the time of the Second Empire (1852-70) it was a semi-official organ of the Government of Napoleon III; it had a sub-title—*Journal de l'Empire*. p. 53

43 *The Morning Post*—daily Conservative newspaper published in London in 1772-1937. In the mid-19th century it was the organ of rightist Whig elements, the followers of Palmerston. p. 56

44 *Saragossa*—city in Spain on the river Ebro. During the Peninsular War Saragossa put up a heroic defence against besieging French forces in 1808-09. (See also Note 32). p. 61

45 By the Danubian quarrel Marx means the diplomatic struggle at the 1856 Paris Congress and later over the question of uniting the Danubian principalities of Moldavia and Wallachia, then under Turkish rule. Hoping to place a member of the Bonaparte dynasty at their head, France suggested that the principalities be joined in a single Rumanian state under the rule of a foreign prince belonging to one of the ruling dynasties of Europe. France was supported by Russia, Prussia and Sardinia. Turkey, which opposed the union because it feared that the Rumanian state would strive to throw off the yoke of the Ottoman Empire, was supported by Austria and Britain. In the long run the Congress acknowledged the need to determine the feeling of the Rumanian population by means of elections to the local Divans. The elections took place, but due to falsifications opponents of the union won out in the Moldavian Divan. This gave rise to protests from France, Russia, Prussia and Sardinia, which demanded that the elections be annulled. Turkey delayed with its reply, and these countries broke off diplomatic relations with it in August 1857. The conflict was settled through the mediation of Napoleon III, who persuaded the British Government not to oppose the French plan, which was equally beneficial to Britain. The elections in the principalities were annulled, but a new elections failed to settle the issue. The question of uniting the two principalities was solved by the Rumanians themselves in 1859. p. 61

46 The German duchies of Holstein and Schleswig were for some centuries under the rule of the Danish crown. The London Treaty guaranteeing the integrity of the Danish monarchy, signed on May 8, 1852, by Russia, Austria, Britain, France, Prussia and Sweden, together with representatives of Denmark, recognised the right of the two duchies to self-government but preserved the supreme rule over them of the Danish King. However, in spite of the treaty, the Danish Government published a constitution in 1855 which abolished the independence and self-government of the German duchies under Danish rule. In retaliation, the German Diet issued a decree in February 1857 protesting against the enforcement of the constitution in the

duchies, but by mistake named only Holstein and Lauenburg (the third German duchy under Danish rule) and failed to mention Schleswig. Denmark took advantage of this and prepared to incorporate Schleswig as its possession, which brought on protests not only from the Schleswig population, which did not want to be separated from Holstein, but also from Prussia, Austria and Britain, which viewed Denmark's action as a violation of the London Treaty. p. 62

47 According to an entry in Marx's notebook for 1857, the article "investigation of Tortures in India" was written by him on August 28, but for some unknown reason the editors of the *New York Daily Tribune* published it after the article"The Indian Revolt"(see this collection, pp. 79-82), to which the editors here refer and which was written by Marx on September 4. p. 63

48 *Blue Books*—the general title of materials and documents published by the British Parliament and the Foreign Office. The Blue Books, so called for their blue covers, have been published in England since the 17th century and are the principal official record of the country's economic and diplomatic history. The author here refers to the Blue Book entitled *East India (Torture)*, London, 1855-57. p. 63

49 *Report of the Commission for the Investigation of Alleged Cases of Torture at Madras*, London, 1855. p. 63

50 *Agramante*—the Moorish king in Ariosto's poem *Orlando Furioso*. At war with Charlemagne, Agramante besieged Paris, concentrating the bulk of his forces by the walls of that city. Marx here refers to the well-known line from *Orlando Furioso*, "There is dissent in Agramante's camp", commonly used to imply dissension. p. 69

51 *The Daily News*—British Liberal newspaper, organ of the industrial bourgeoisie; appeared under this title in London from 1846 to 1930. p. 69

52 *The Mofussilite*—a weekly Liberal English-language newspaper which appeared in India after 1845, first in Meerut and later in Agra and Ambala. p. 72

53 The author refers to the East India Company Charter of 1853. (See Note 3.) p. 75

54 In the *Vendée* (a province in western France) the French royalists utilised the backward peasantry to engineer a counter-revolutionary revolt in 1793. It was crushed by the republican army, whose soldiers were known as the "Blues".

The *Spanish guerrillas*—participants of the guerrilla war during the national-liberation struggle of the Spanish people against the French invaders in 1808-14. The peasantry, which stubbornly resisted the conquerors, was the principal motive force behind the guerrilla.

The *Serbian* and *Croat* troops took part in crushing the revolutionary movement in Hungary and Austria during the revolution of 1848-49. The *Garde mobile* was established by a French Government decree of February 25, 1848, to suppress the revolutionary masses. Its detachments, chiefly composed of de-classed elements, were used to quell the uprising of Paris workers in June 1848. General Cavaignac, being the Minister of War, personally commanded the massacre of the workers.

Decembrists—a secret Bonapartist society founded in 1849. Consisted predominantly of de-classed elements, political adventurers, militarists, etc. Its members facilitated the election of Louis Bonaparte as President of the

French Republic on December 10, 1848 (whence the name of the society), and took part in the *coup d'état* of December 2, 1851, which led to louis Bonaparte being proclaimed Emperor of France as Napoleon III in 1852. They were active organisers of mass repressions of republicans and particularly of participants of the 1848 revolution. p. 79

55 The author refers to the First Opium War (1839-42)—Britain's aggressive war against China, which marked the beginning of China's semi-colonial status. The destruction in Canton by the Chinese authorities of opium stocks belonging to foreign merchants served as a pretext for the war. Taking advantage of the defeat suffered by backward feudal China, the British colonialists saddled it with the predacious Nanking Treaty (August 29, 1842), which opened five Chinese ports (Canton, Amoy, Foochow, Ningpo, and Shanghai) to British trade, transferred the island of Hong Kong into Britain's "eternal possession", and stipulated a tremendous war contribution by China. Under a supplementary protocol of 1843 China was also made to grant foreigners extraterritorial rights. p. 80

56 The author refers to the barbarous bombardment of Canton on orders of the British superintendent in China, John Bowring, in which nearly 5,000 houses were destroyed in the city suburbs. The bombardment was a prologue to the Second Opium War of 1856-58. (See Note 29).

Peace Society—a bourgeois pacifist organisation founded in 1816 in London by the Quakers. The society enjoyed vigorous support from the Free Traders, who thought that given peace Britain would through Free Trade make better use of its industrial superiority and thus achieve economic and political supremacy.

During the suppression of the uprising in Algeria in 1845, General Pelissier, later marshal of France, ordered the asphyxiation by the smoke of camp-fires of a thousand Arab rebels hiding in mountain caves. p. 81

57 The author refers to Gaius Julius Caesar's *Commentarii de bello Gallico*. The fact here cited is from Book 8, written by Caesar's former legate and friend A. Hirtius, who continued his notes on the Gallic War. p. 81

58 Marx alluded to the criminal code of Charles V (*Constitutio criminalis Carolina*) adopted by the Reichstag at Regensburg in 1532. The code was known for its extreme severity. p. 81

59 W. Blackstone, *Commentaries on the Laws of England*, Vols. I-IV, First Edition, London, 1765-69. p. 81

60 Mozart's *Die Entführung aus dem Serail*, Act III, Scene 6, aria by Osmin. p. 82

61 According to the biblical tale, the Israelites destroyed the walls of Jericho with the blast of their trumpets. p. 82

62 The editors of the *New-York Daily Tribune*, who inserted this phrase, alluded to their staff correspondent, the Hungarian writer and journalist Ferencz Pulszky, who emigrated from Hungary after the defeat of the 1848 revolution. Pulszky contributed reviews chiefy on international subjects. p. 83

63 Marx evidently refers to *The Calcutta Gazette*, an English newspaper published in Bengal from 1784. It was the official organ of the British Government in India. p. 84

[64] The author refers to the first *Anglo-Afghan War* of 1838-42, which Britain started with the purpose of subjugating Afghanistan. In August 1839 the British captured Kabul, but were compelled to withdraw in January 1842 owing to an uprising which broke out in November 1841. They turned back towards India, their retreat culminating in panicky flight. Just one out of the 4,500 British soldiers and 12,000 camp followers reached the Indian border. p. 86

[65] The author refers to the British naval expedition to the mouth of the Schelde River in 1809 during the war against Napoleonic France. After seizing the island of Walcheren, the British failed to develop the action and were forced to withdraw after losing nearly 10,000 men of their 40,000 landing force from hunger and disease. p. 87

[66] In the *New-York Daily Tribune* this article begins with the phrase: "We yesterday received files of London journals up to the 7th inst.", which was put in by the editors. p. 91

[67] *The Morning Advertiser*—British daily newspaper founded in London in 1794; in the 1850's it was an organ of the radical bourgeoisie. p. 94

[68] *The Friend of India*—British newspaper founded in Serampore in 1818; in the 1850's it appeared once a week and was of a bourgeois liberal trend. p. 96

[69] *The Military Spectator*—British military weekly newspaper which appeared in London from 1857 to 1858. p. 96

[70] *The Bombay Courier*—British government newspaper, organ of the East India Company; founded in 1790. p. 98

[71] This table, compiled by Marx, was sent by him to New York seemingly together with the given article, but was printed by the editors separately in the same issue of the newspaper on page 6. p. 99

[72] The author refers to the Crimean War. On November 5, 1854, at Inkerman, Russian troops counter-attacked the troops of the Anglo-Franco-Turkish coalition with the purpose of thwarting an attack prepared against Sevastopol. In spite of the bravery of the Russian troops, the Anglo-Franco-Turkish forces won the battle. p. 101

[73] On October 25, 1854, a battle took place at Balaklava between the Russian and allied forces, in which the British and French suffered tremendous losses in spite of their advantageous position. Mistakes of the British command led to the loss of a British light cavalry brigade. p. 102

[74] *The Bombay Gazette*—British newspaper in India founded in 1791. p. 103

[75] *Globe*—abbreviated title of the British daily newspaper *The Globe and Traveller*, published in London from 1803. Whig organ, it was a government newspaper whenever the Whigs were in power. Since 1866 an organ of the Conservatives. p. 107

[76] The author refers to the Act of Parliament of 1833 which deprived the East India Company of its trading monopoly in China and abolished it as a trading agency. Parliament left the Company its administrative functions and prolonged its Charter to 1853. p. 108

77 *The Phoenix*—British government newspaper in India; published in Calcutta from 1856 to 1861. p. 109

78 The title is given in accordance with an entry in Marx's notebook of 1858. p. 111

79 The author refers to the Crimean War of 1853-56. The battle at Alma took place on September 20, 1854, and was won by the allied army. p. 111

80 The reference is to the Crimean War of 1853-56. During an abortive attack by the allies on the third bastion of the fortifications at Sevastopol (the so-called Big Redan) on June 18, 1855, Windham was in command of the brigade. p. 111

81 The title accords with the entry in Marx's notebook for 1858. p. 117

82 The reference is to the first Anglo-Afghan War of 1838-42. (See Note 64). p. 118

83 Engels refers to an ancient type of fortification erected in Burma round towns and camps. p. 125

84 The Spanish fortress of *Badajoz*, held by the French, was captured by the British under Wellington on April 6, 1812.

The French-held Spanish fortress of *San-Sebastian* was attacked on August 31, 1813. p. 126

85 The reference is to the proclamation issued by Lord Canning, Governor-General of India, on March 3, 1858, according to which the dominions of the Kingdom of Oudh, including lands of the big feudal landowners, the talukdars, who had joined the revolt, were confiscated by the British authorities. However, the British Government, which sought to win the talukdars to its side, changed the sense of Canning's proclamation. The talukdars were promised inviolability of their possessions, after which they betrayed the revolt and went over to the British side.

A critical analysis of the proclamation is made by Marx in his articles "The Annexation of Oudh" and "Lord Canning's Proclamation and Land Tenure in India". (See this collection, pp. 129-34 and pp. 135-38). p. 127

86 In spite of the fine organisation of their army, which fought against the British with stubborn bravery, the Sikhs were defeated in battles at the village of Mudki (near Ferozepore) on December 18, 1845, at Ferozeshah on December 21, 1845, and at the village of Aliwal near Ludhiana on January 28, 1846. As a result, the Sikhs lost the first Anglo-Sikh War of 1845-46. The chief cause of the defeat was treachery on the part of their supreme command. p. 128

87 The title is given in accordance with Marx's notebook for 1858. p. 129

88 Marx quotes the proclamation of Governor-General Lord Canning concerning Oudh (see Note 85), published in *The Times* on May 8, 1858. p. 129

89 The reference is to the suppression by Russian reactionaries of the revolt of 1830-31 in the Polish Kingdom which was part of the Russian Empire. p. 129

90 The author refers to the Austro-Italian War of 1848-49, in which the forces of the Sardinian King Charles Albert suffered a severe defeat in the battle of Novara (Northern Italy) on March 23, 1849. p. 129

91 Oudh had been part of the Mogul Empire, but in the mid-18th century the Mogul Viceroy in Oudh became in fact an independent ruler. The English in 1765 turned Oudh into a subsidiary principality subject to Britain. Political power virtually passed into the hands of the British Resident. To camouflage this state of affairs the English often styled the ruler of Oudh as King. p. 130

92 In accordance with the treaty concluded between the East India Company and the nabob of Oudh in 1801, Wellesley, the Governor-General of India, annexed half the nabob's possessions under the pretext of his failing to pay his debts. This involved Gorakhpur, Rohilkhand and some of the territory between the rivers Ganges and Jumna. p. 130

93 The editors of the *New-York Daily Tribune*, who made this insertion in Marx's article, refer to the correspondence between Indian Governor-General Lord Canning and Outram, the Chief Commissioner of Oudh, concerning Canning's proclamation in relation to Oudh, (see Note 85), which was published in that newspaper on June 5, 1858. p. 135

94 Almost all India was under British rule by the middle of the 19th century. Cashmere, Rajputana, part of Hyderabad, Mysore and some other smaller principalities were vassals of the East India Company. p. 135

95 The reference is to the Act of 1793 on Permanent Zemindari, issued by Indian Governor-General Cornwallis. (See note 22.) p. 136

96 In his dispatch of April 19, 1858, President of the Board of Control, Lord Ellenborough, referred critically to Lord Canning's proclamation in relation to Oudh. (See Note 85.) In view of the fact that Lord Ellenborough's dispatch was disapproved of in British political circles, he was compelled to resign. p. 138

97 The reference is to the Bill tabled in Parliament by the Derby Ministry in March and adopted in July 1858. The Bill became a law under the title "Act for the Better Government of India". Under this law India came fully under the Crown, while the East India Company was dissolved, with £3 million in compensation payable to its shareholders. The President of the dissolved Board of Control was replaced by a Secretary of State for India and his consultative organ—the Indian Council. The Governor-General of India was named the Viceroy, remaining in effect the executive of the will of the Secretary for India in London.

A critical analysis of the act is presented by Marx in his article "The Indian Bill". (See this collection, pp. 156-59.) p. 146

98 The title is according to Marx's notebook for 1858. p. 151

99 The reference is to the colonial wars conducted by the French colonialists in Algeria in the 1830s-1870s with the purpose of conquering the country. The French invasion of Algeria was long and stubbornly resisted by the Arab population. The French waged the war with extreme brutality. By 1847 the conquest of Algeria was in the main completed, but the struggle of the Algerian people for their independence never really ceased. p. 154

100 The title accords with Marx's notebook for 1858. p. 156

101 The author refers to the Regulating Act of 1773. The Act reduced the number of shareholders entitled to participate in deliberating the affairs of the Company and to elect the Court of Directors. Under the Act only shareholders with not less than £1,000 worth of shares had the right to vote at meetings of shareholders. The first time the Governor-General of India and

the members of his Council were appointed individually for a five-year term and could be dismissed only by the King on representation of the Court of Directors of the Company. Subsequently the Governor-General and his Council were to have been nominated by the company. Under the 1773 Act a Supreme Court was instituted in Calcutta consisting of Lord Chief Justice and three judges. p. 156

102 The *Bill on Foreigners* (or Conspiracy Bill) was proposed by Palmerston in the House of Commons on February 8, 1858, under pressure of the French Government (Palmerston announced his intention to table the Bill on February 5). Under this Bill any individual residing within the United Kingdom, be he a British subject or foreigner, was to be tried by a British court and severely punished if found guilty of organising or participating in a conspiracy designed to assassinate any person in Britain or any other country. Under pressure of a mass movement of protest the Bill was rejected by the House of Commons, and Palmerston was compelled to resign. p. 158

103 After the Ministry of Derby came to power the President of the Board of Control, Lord Ellenborough, was authorised to work out a reform Bill to improve the government of India. However, his Bill did not satisfy the government because of its much too complicated system of electing the Indian Council. The Bill was strongly opposed and rejected. p. 158

104 *Civis Romanus sum*—the nickname Palmerston was given after his speech in the House of Commons on June 25, 1850, concerning the case of the merchant Pacifico. In justification of the acts of the British Navy, which was sent to Greece in order to protect a British subject of Portuguese descent, a merchant Don Pacifico (whose home was burned in Athens), Palmerston declared that like the formula of Roman citizenship, *civis Romanus sum*, which secured universal respect for the citizens of ancient Rome, so too British citizenship should guarantee the security of British subjects wherever they may be. Palmerston's chauvinistic speech was met jubilantly by the English bourgeoisie. p. 159

105 The reference is to the Anglo-Burmese War of 1852. (See Note 19.) p. 165

106 This and the following pages, to which Marx refers in the text of his notes, are from: Robert Sewell, *The Analytical History of India from the Earliest Times to the Abolition of the Honourable East India Company in 1858*, London, 1870. p. 168

107 *Guardian*—abbreviated title of the bourgeois *Manchester Guardian*, organ of the Free Traders, later of the Liberal Party. Founded in Manchester in 1821. p. 178

108 *The Examiner*—English bourgeois liberal weekly, appeared in London in 1808-81. p. 178

109 *Neue Rheinische Zeitung. Organ der Democratie*—appeared daily in Cologne from June 1, 1848, to May 19, 1849. The editor was Marx. The editorial board included Engels. The paper was a militant organ of the proletarian wing of the democratic movement and contributed greatly to bringing up the masses, and rallying them to the fight against the counter-revolution. The editorials, which mirrored the attitude of the newspaper to the key issues of the German and European revolution, were as a rule written by Marx and Engels. In face of police persecutions the paper took a courageous stand on behalf of the interests of the revolutionary democrats

and the proletariat. Marx's deportation and repressions against the other editors of the *Neue Rheinische Zeitung* caused the paper to close down.

p. 180

110 The author refers to the unequal Tientsin Treaty signed by Britain and China in June 1858. It ended the Second Opium War of 1856-58. The treaty opened new ports for foreign trade along the Yangtse River, in Manchuria, the islands of Taiwan and Hainan, and the port of Tientsin. Permanent foreign diplomatic representatives were admitted to Peking. Foreigners were granted the right of free travel throughout the country and of coastal and river shipping. The safety of missionaries was guaranteed. p. 182

Name Index

D

E

F

G

N

O

P

R

S

Z

Geographical index *

* The Index contains geographical names associated with the national-liberation uprising of 1857-59 in India. - Ed.